I0448469

January 2013

CUBA DEMOCRACY ASSISTANCE

USAID's Program Is Improved, but State Could Better Monitor Its Implementing Partners

G A O

Accountability ★ Integrity ★ Reliability

GAO-13-285

CUBA DEMOCRACY ASSISTANCE

USAID's Program Is Improved, but State Could Better Monitor Its Implementing Partners

Highlights of GAO-13-285, a report to the Chairman, Committee on Foreign Relations, U.S. Senate

Why GAO Did This Study

Since 1996, Congress has appropriated $205 million to USAID and State to support democracy assistance for Cuba. Because of Cuban government restrictions, conditions in Cuba pose security risks to the implementing partners—primarily NGOs—and subpartners that provide U.S. assistance.

For this report, GAO (1) identified current assistance, implementing partners, subpartners, and beneficiaries; (2) reviewed USAID's and State's efforts to implement the program in accordance with U.S. laws and regulations and to address program risks; and (3) examined USAID's and State's monitoring of the use of program funds. This report is a publicly releasable version of a Sensitive But Unclassified Report that GAO issued in December 2012.

To address these objectives, GAO analyzed program activities and funding, relevant laws and regulations, and practices for monitoring the use of funds. GAO also conducted performance and financial reviews of a nongeneralizable sample of six implementing partners—representing about 60 percent of USAID and State funding for awards and contracts active in fiscal year 2011—and 11 subpartners.

What GAO Recommends

GAO is recommending that State take steps to improve its financial monitoring of implementing partners and provide clear guidance for approving subpartners. State concurred with GAO's recommendations and cited steps they are taking to address them.

View GAO-13-285. For more information, contact David Gootnick at (202) 512-3149 or gootnickd@gao.gov.

What GAO Found

The U.S. Agency for International Development (USAID) and Department of State (State) provide democracy assistance for Cuba aimed at developing civil society and promoting freedom of information. Typical program beneficiaries include Cuban community leaders, independent journalists, women, youths, and marginalized groups. USAID receives the majority of funding allocated for this assistance, although State has received 32 percent of funding since 2004. In recent years, both USAID and State have provided more funding for program implementation to for-profit and nongovernmental organizations (NGO) with a worldwide or regional focus than to universities and to NGOs that focus only on Cuba. All types of implementing partners, but worldwide or regional organizations in particular, used subpartners to implement program activities under 21 of the 29 awards and contracts that GAO reviewed.

USAID and State legal officials view the Cuba democracy program's authorizing legislation as allowing the agencies discretion in determining the types of activities that can be funded with program assistance. Agency officials added that the agencies ensure that program activities directly relate to democracy promotion as broadly illustrated in related program legislation. The officials stated that organizations are expected to work with agency program officers to determine what activities are permitted or appropriate. In addition, they said that program partners and subpartners are expected to spend U.S. government funds consistent with U.S. laws, and that requirements in primary award agreements generally flow down to any subpartners.

USAID has improved its performance and financial monitoring of implementing partners' use of program funds by implementing new policies and hiring contractors to improve monitoring and evaluation and to conduct financial internal controls reviews, but GAO found gaps in State's financial monitoring. While GAO found some gaps in implementing partners' performance planning and reporting, both agencies are taking steps to improve performance monitoring. For financial monitoring, USAID performs financial internal controls reviews of its implementing partners with the assistance of an external auditor. Since 2008, USAID has used a risk-based approach to determine the coverage and frequency of the 30 reviews the auditor has conducted, which have identified weaknesses in implementing partners' financial management, procurement, and internal controls. However, because of resource constraints, State did not perform financial internal controls reviews for more than two-thirds of its implementing partners during fiscal years 2010 through 2012. State procured an external financial auditor in September 2012 that plans to review more than half of State's implementing partners, and has taken steps toward implementing a risk-based approach for scheduling these reviews. Federal regulations generally require agencies to approve the use of subpartners. GAO found that USAID issued specific guidance in 2011 to its implementing partners on requirements for subpartner approval. While State told GAO it has similar requirements, State's requirements are not clearly specified in its written guidance. As a result, State was not provided with the information it would have needed to approve at least 91 subawards and subcontracts that were obligated under eight awards.

Contents

Abbreviations

DRL	Bureau of Democracy, Human Rights, and Labor
LAC	Latin American and Caribbean Bureau
M/E	Monitoring and evaluation
NED	National Endowment for Democracy
NGO	Nongovernmental organization
OMB	Office of Management and Budget
OTI	Office of Transition Initiatives
Partner	Implementing partner
RFA	Request for Application
RFP	Request for Proposal
State	Department of State
USAID	United States Agency for International Development
USINT	U.S. Interests Section in Havana, Cuba
WHA	Bureau of Western Hemisphere Affairs

United States Government Accountability Office
Washington, DC 20548

January 25, 2013

The Honorable John F. Kerry
Chairman
Committee on Foreign Relations
United States Senate

Dear Mr. Chairman:

The U.S. Agency for International Development (USAID) and the Department of State (State) provide assistance to increase respect for human rights and fundamental freedoms, strengthen independent Cuban civil society, and foster greater access to independent information on the island.[1] Cubans have lived under an authoritarian regime for more than 50 years; in that time, Cubans have faced continuous restrictions in citizens' rights to organize, express themselves freely, and participate in political life without fear of being harassed and repressed by the Cuban government. Conditions in Cuba pose risks and challenges for the delivery of program assistance on the island, which is largely provided by implementing partners (partners) and their subpartners.[2] In fiscal years 1996 through 2011, Congress appropriated $205 million for Cuba democracy assistance, with about 90 percent of program funding provided since fiscal year 2004. While USAID has received most of this funding, State has also received program funding allocations since fiscal year 2004.

---

[1]The Cuban Democracy Act of 1992 (Pub. L. No. 102-484, Div. A, Tit. XVII) and the Cuban Liberty and Democratic Solidarity (LIBERTAD) Act of 1996 (Pub. L. No. 104-114, commonly known as the Helms-Burton Act) authorize assistance and other support for individuals and independent nongovernmental organizations (NGOs) to promote peaceful, nonviolent democratic change in Cuba through various types of democracy-building efforts. Appropriations are provided through the annual Department of State, Foreign Operations, and Related Programs Appropriations Act, generally in the Economic Support Fund account.

[2]For the purposes of our review, partners include contractors, grantees, and recipients of cooperative agreements. Awardees include recipients of grants and cooperative agreements. Subpartners include recipients of subawards (subgrants, grants under contract, consultants, etc.) and subcontracts. Program beneficiaries are the ultimate targets of program assistance, including human rights and democracy advocates on the island, as well as Cuban civil society actors.

In November 2006 and November 2008, we reported problems with USAID's management and oversight of its Cuba program, such as oversight weaknesses that increased the risk of grantees' improper use of grant funds and noncompliance with U.S. laws and regulations.[3] We made several recommendations to help USAID strengthen its program management and monitoring, including recommendations to improve the timeliness of preaward reviews, and to ensure partners develop approved implementation plans for awards. USAID has reported taking several steps to address the recommendations. However, security risks and challenges related to the delivery of program assistance persist.

To respond to your request, this report focuses on USAID's and State's efforts to provide democracy assistance for Cuba. We (1) identified the types and amounts of assistance that USAID and State have provided, as well as characteristics of their partners, subpartners, and program beneficiaries; (2) reviewed USAID's and State's efforts to implement the program in accordance with U.S. laws and regulations and to address program risks; and (3) examined USAID's and State's monitoring of the use of program funds. This report is a publicly releasable version of a prior GAO report, issued in December 2012, that USAID and State had designated Sensitive But Unclassified. Although the information provided in this report is more limited in scope, it addresses the same questions and uses the same overall methodology as the sensitive report.

In conducting this review, we identified all awards and contracts funded from 1996 to 2012 and analyzed selected characteristics of all 22 USAID and State partners that received program funding from fiscal years 2007 to 2009 appropriations and were active in fiscal year 2011. These partners received 29 awards and contracts during that period. We reviewed relevant U.S. laws and regulations and agency and departmental policies and procedures, and we interviewed USAID and State officials regarding program implementation and related risks. We also analyzed reported activities, assistance delivered, and management

---

[3]See GAO, *Foreign Assistance: U.S. Democracy Assistance for Cuba Needs Better Management and Oversight*, GAO-07-147 (Washington, D.C.: Nov. 15, 2006); and GAO, *Foreign Assistance: Continued Efforts Needed to Strengthen USAID's Oversight of U.S. Democracy Assistance for Cuba*, GAO-09-165 (Washington, D.C.: Nov. 24, 2008). These reports focused primarily on assistance provided by USAID's Latin American and Caribbean Bureau. A classified version of the November 2006 report was published in May 2007.

and internal controls[4] for a nonprobability,[5] nongeneralizable sample of six USAID and State partners and 11 of their subpartners, to assess performance and financial monitoring and oversight of their awards and contracts. We selected at least one partner from each of the four USAID and State bureaus and offices implementing program assistance. The six selected partners were among the top 15 recipients of program funding awarded in fiscal years 2007 through 2010 and represented about 60 percent of funding for awards active in fiscal year 2011. These six partners received 10 USAID and State awards and contracts over the time period we reviewed—five from USAID and five from State. We reviewed and analyzed performance and financial documentation and data and conducted interviews with USAID and State officials and with representatives of partners and subpartners in our sample. In addition, we conducted fieldwork in Miami, Florida, where we interviewed representatives and reviewed documentation at local partners and subpartners, and at the U.S. Interests Section (USINT) in Havana, Cuba, where we interviewed U.S. officials and observed activities at post.[6] Appendix I provides further details on our scope and methodology.

We conducted this performance audit from September 2011 to January 2013 in accordance with generally accepted government auditing standards. Those standards require that we plan and perform the audit to obtain sufficient, appropriate evidence to provide a reasonable basis for our findings and conclusions based on our audit objectives. We believe that the evidence obtained provides a reasonable basis for our findings and conclusions based on our audit objectives.

---

[4]Internal controls comprise the plans, methods, and procedures used to meet missions, goals, and objectives and, in doing so, support performance-based management.

[5]A nonprobability sample is not randomly selected, but rather is selected based on the use of a set of key criteria; also, it is not a large enough sample for findings to be generalizable to the full population of partners.

[6]The United States does not have an embassy in Cuba, but USINT provides services including consular services and public diplomacy.

GAO-13-285 Cuba Democracy Assistance

Background

Challenges Affecting Cuba Democracy Assistance

Conditions in Cuba continue to pose substantial challenges for U.S. assistance. Cuba is a Communist state that restricts nearly all political dissent on the island; tactics for suppressing dissent in Cuba include surveillance, arbitrary arrests, detentions, travel restrictions, exile, criminal prosecutions, and loss of employment. Furthermore, there is no free press in Cuba, and independent journalists and activists are harassed and imprisoned. The Cuban government substantially restricts and controls the flow of information, limiting access to the Internet, cell phones, radio antennas, and other items, and restricting their use through high costs, punitive laws, and the threat of confiscation. Moreover, the government routinely jams all external, non-Cuban broadcasts, including the U.S. government-supported Radio and TV Martí broadcasts.

The United States, which maintains an embargo on most trade with Cuba, does not have diplomatic relations with the Cuban government. Consequently, USAID does not work cooperatively or collaboratively with Cuban government agencies, as it does in most other countries receiving U.S. democracy assistance. USAID does not have staff in Cuba, and State does not have staff dedicated to the Cuba democracy program in Havana.[7] USAID and State program staff have been unable to obtain visas to visit Cuba over the past decade, which poses challenges for program implementation, monitoring, and evaluation. In addition, Cuban law prohibits citizens from cooperating with U.S. democracy assistance activities. In December 2009, a subcontractor working for one of USAID's partners was arrested in Cuba while delivering computer equipment to provide Internet access to Jewish communities on the island. He was subsequently sentenced to 15 years in prison for "acts against the independence or the territorial integrity of the state."

Roles and Responsibilities for Implementing Cuba Democracy Assistance

Several USAID and State bureaus and offices implement Cuba democracy assistance efforts, including soliciting proposals, competitively awarding funds, and monitoring program implementation.

---

[7]However, staff at USINT have a role in overseeing program efforts that are funded by State's Bureau of Western Hemisphere Affairs.

- USAID:
  - **The Latin American and Caribbean Bureau (LAC), Office of Cuban Affairs**, is chiefly responsible for implementing Cuba democracy assistance efforts.
  - **The Management Bureau** has various offices that also assist in overseeing program awards and contracts.
  - **The Office of Transition Initiatives (OTI)** oversaw implementation of a single contract from fiscal years 2009 through 2012. OTI's Cuba program efforts were envisioned from their inception to be temporary, as is typically the case with OTI's programs, which generally aim to provide short-term assistance.

- State:
  - **The Bureau of Democracy, Human Rights, and Labor (DRL)** is responsible for managing and overseeing the majority of State's Cuba democracy assistance program activities.
  - **The Bureau of Western Hemisphere Affairs (WHA),** including the U.S. Interests Section in Havana, Cuba, (USINT), also manages and oversees Cuba program activities.,
  - **The Bureau of Administration** assists DRL and WHA in the financial management and oversight of Cuba democracy assistance awards.[8]

Reporting on Cuba democracy assistance in 2006,[9] we found that USINT delivered some assistance to independent groups and individuals in Cuba, including assistance provided by USAID- and State-funded awardees. Because of heightened security concerns, USINT no longer has a role in implementing assistance for USAID and State/DRL partners. However, USINT continues to provide information on conditions in Cuba, facilitates and assists with State/WHA training courses, and supports civil society in Cuba.

Table 1 outlines key USAID and State roles and responsibilities for providing U.S. democracy assistance for Cuba.

---

[8]The Office of Acquisitions Management is the primary office within the Bureau of Administration involved in these functions. In addition, there are other bureaus and offices that have administrative and oversight functions for State's Cuba program.

[9]GAO-07-147.

Table 1: Key USAID and State Roles and Responsibilities for Cuba Democracy Assistance

Responsible entity	Staff roles/responsibilities
USAID	
LAC, Office of Cuban Affairs	A Director, four Program Managers, a Budget Analyst, and an Administrative Assistant share full-time responsibilities for program management and oversight. These responsibilities include program design, implementation, and monitoring as well as budgeting and financial management.
Management Bureau	Various staff members assist in program oversight, including closing out awards and contracts, conducting risk assessments, and auditing programs.
OTI	A Country Representative dedicated full-time to Cuba and a part-time Deputy Team Leader shared responsibilities for all aspects of the temporary program's management and oversight through the end of program efforts in fiscal year 2012.
State	
DRL	Two Program Officers share part-time responsibilities for Cuba program planning, implementation, monitoring and evaluation. A Foreign Affairs Officer also provides part-time assistance, primarily on policy issues related to Cuba.
WHA	About a dozen staff members each spend about 5 to 10 percent of their time on Cuba program management and oversight.
USINT, Havana	Several staff, dedicated part-time to providing information on conditions in Cuba, facilitate and assist with State/WHA training courses and support civil society in Cuba.
Bureau of Administration	Various staff members are responsible for financial oversight and providing financial management guidance to DRL and WHA Cuba program partners.

Source: GAO analysis of USAID, State, and other records.

In addition, the National Endowment for Democracy (NED), an independent, nongovernmental organization, funds programs to promote democracy in Cuba through both direct congressional appropriations and with funding that it receives through State/DRL.[10]

Program partners—such as nongovernmental organizations, universities, and development contractors—and subpartners also have roles and responsibilities for Cuba democracy program assistance. USAID and State provide funding for partners through various mechanisms, including grants and cooperative agreements (together referred to as "awards" in this report) and contracts. Partners may also award funding to subpartners to assist them in implementing program efforts. Subpartners

---

[10]NED was not included in the scope of this review, because it is not a U.S. government agency and because USAID and State provide the majority of Cuba democracy assistance.

may include consultants, subcontractors, subgrantees, and recipients of grants under contract.

USAID and State Focus on Promoting Cuban Civil Society and Access to Information; Most Funding Goes to Worldwide or Regional Partners and Their Subpartners

USAID and State support democracy for Cuba by providing awards and contracts to partners with objectives related to developing civil society and promoting freedom of information. USAID receives the majority of funding allocated for this assistance, although State has received 32 percent of funding since it started taking part in the program in 2004. Since 2008, USAID and State have awarded more funds to larger organizations with a worldwide or regional presence than to the other two categories of typical awardees: universities, and smaller organizations that focus only on Cuba. Under 21 of the 29 recent awards and contracts that we reviewed, partners used subpartners to implement program activities and obligated about 40 percent of the funding associated with these awards and contracts to subpartners. Worldwide or regional organizations provided more than 90 percent of the funding provided to subpartners.

Program Focuses on Promoting Civil Society and Access to Information

USAID's and State's democracy assistance efforts for Cuba generally focus on developing an independent civil society and promoting freedom of information in Cuba. The overall goal and guiding principle of U.S. democracy assistance for Cuba is to improve the effectiveness of citizens to participate in activities affecting their lives and to increase access to information.[11] Efforts to develop Cuban civil society include training in organizational and community development, leadership, and advocacy. Related material assistance may include the provision of books, pamphlets, movies, music, and other materials that promote democratic values. In addition, efforts to promote freedom of information have included the following, among other activities:

- information technology training for Cuban nationals, ranging from basic computing to blogging;

---

[11]The overall goal of the Cuba program is laid out in USAID and State's most recent performance plan report for fiscal year 2011. This report also notes that the Cuba program is focused on advancing democracy and improving human rights conditions by supporting efforts to promote democratic reforms in Cuba, and promoting increased respect for human rights and fundamental freedoms in Cuba. State officials noted that State/DRL Cuba program efforts focus on civil society and human rights, including freedom of information as well as workers' and women's rights.

- journalism training;
- support for independent publications; and
- provision of material assistance.

USAID and State officials noted that in recent years, program efforts have included a greater focus on information technology, particularly on supporting independent bloggers and developing social networking platforms on the island.

Several partners we reviewed received funding to support international solidarity activities, although agency and partner officials indicated that the program recently has reduced its focus on off-island activities to foster support for democracy in Cuba. Activities of this type that State/DRL funded in fiscal years 2009 through 2011 included the following:

- an essay contest for Latin American youths related to Cuba Solidarity Day, and
- exhibits and documentaries presented outside Cuba for the purpose of bringing awareness globally to Cuban human rights issues and civil society development.

In recent years, USAID and State had few awards or contracts focused solely on such humanitarian assistance as assistance for political prisoners and their families, according to agency officials. USINT officials noted that humanitarian assistance has declined along with a decrease in the number of political prisoners in Cuba.[12] Officials added that USINT itself no longer provides any humanitarian assistance on the island.

To broaden reach and impact, Cuba democracy assistance efforts have expanded beyond a focus on traditional activists to include groups such as poor and rural communities, religious organizations, small businesses, and information technology enthusiasts. Typical program beneficiaries also include Cuban community leaders, independent journalists, independent bloggers, women, and youths.

---

[12]USINT officials noted that, during a crackdown in 2003 known as the "Black Spring," the Cuban government arrested 75 dissidents. All of the dissidents have since been released, with many exiled to Spain. According to the USINT officials, in the past 2 to 3 years the Cuban government has shifted away from sentencing convicted dissidents to long prison terms; instead, the government now is generally detaining dissidents for shorter periods of time. Officials added that as of January 2012 there were several dozen political prisoners in Cuba, but that it is difficult to ascertain exact numbers as there are no official statistics.

Table 2 summarizes information on recent program assistance and target beneficiaries.

Table 2: Cuba Democracy Assistance Provided from Fiscal Years 2009 to 2011

Purpose of assistance	Examples of assistance provided	Target beneficiaries
Development of independent civil society	• Training on topics such as democracy building, economic rights, free markets, leadership and advocacy, organizational and community development, conducting small projects, and human rights abuse response and documentation • Books, pamphlets, and other materials to promote democratic values • Support for the development of independent social networking platforms • Technical and material assistance to increase awareness of freedom of expression.	Community leaders Cuban youths and students, girls and women, poor and rural communities Other groups
Promotion of freedom of information	• Information technology training, such as basic computing, Internet, and blogging • Journalism training • Digital newspaper publication to disseminate work of independent journalists • Development and distribution of media content for youth • Digital photo contest • Shortwave independent radio station • Material assistance	Cuban public Independent Cuban journalists Cuban youths
Humanitarian assistance	• Food products, over-the-counter medication, basic clothing • Financial aid for family members of political prisoners • Material assistance for civil society organizations targeting political prisoners and their families	Political prisoners and their families

Source: GAO analysis of USAID, State, and other records.

USAID Has Received the Majority of Allocations, but State's Portion Has Grown in Recent Years

In fiscal years 1996 through 2011, Congress appropriated $205 million for Cuba democracy assistance, appropriating 87 percent of these funds since 2004. Increased funding for Cuba democracy assistance was recommended by the interagency Commission for Assistance to a Free Cuba, which was established by President George W. Bush in 2003.[13] Program funding, which peaked in 2008 with appropriations totaling $44.4 million, has ranged between $15 and $20 million per year during fiscal years 2009 through 2012. For fiscal year 2013, USAID and State reduced their combined funding request to $15 million, citing operational challenges to assistance efforts in Cuba.[14]

In fiscal years 1996 through 2011, $138.2 million of Cuba democracy funds were allocated to USAID and $52.3 million were allocated to State (see fig. 1).[15]

---

[13]President Bush established the Commission for Assistance to a Free Cuba in October 2003 to identify (1) ways in which the U.S. government could hasten the end of the Castro dictatorship and (2) U.S. programs to assist the Cuban people during a transition to democracy. The commission's July 2006 report recommended providing $80 million over 2 years to increase support for Cuban civil society, disseminate uncensored information to Cuba, expand international awareness of conditions in Cuba, and help realize a democratic transition in Cuba. The report also recommended subsequent annual funding of at least $20 million until the end of the Castro regime.

[14]State officials stated that they do not believe this reduction will affect program efficacy.

[15]The agencies have obligated 81 percent of these funds to partner organizations to implement program assistance; the agencies used the remainder of funding for expenses such as program administration and procurement of materials for distribution.

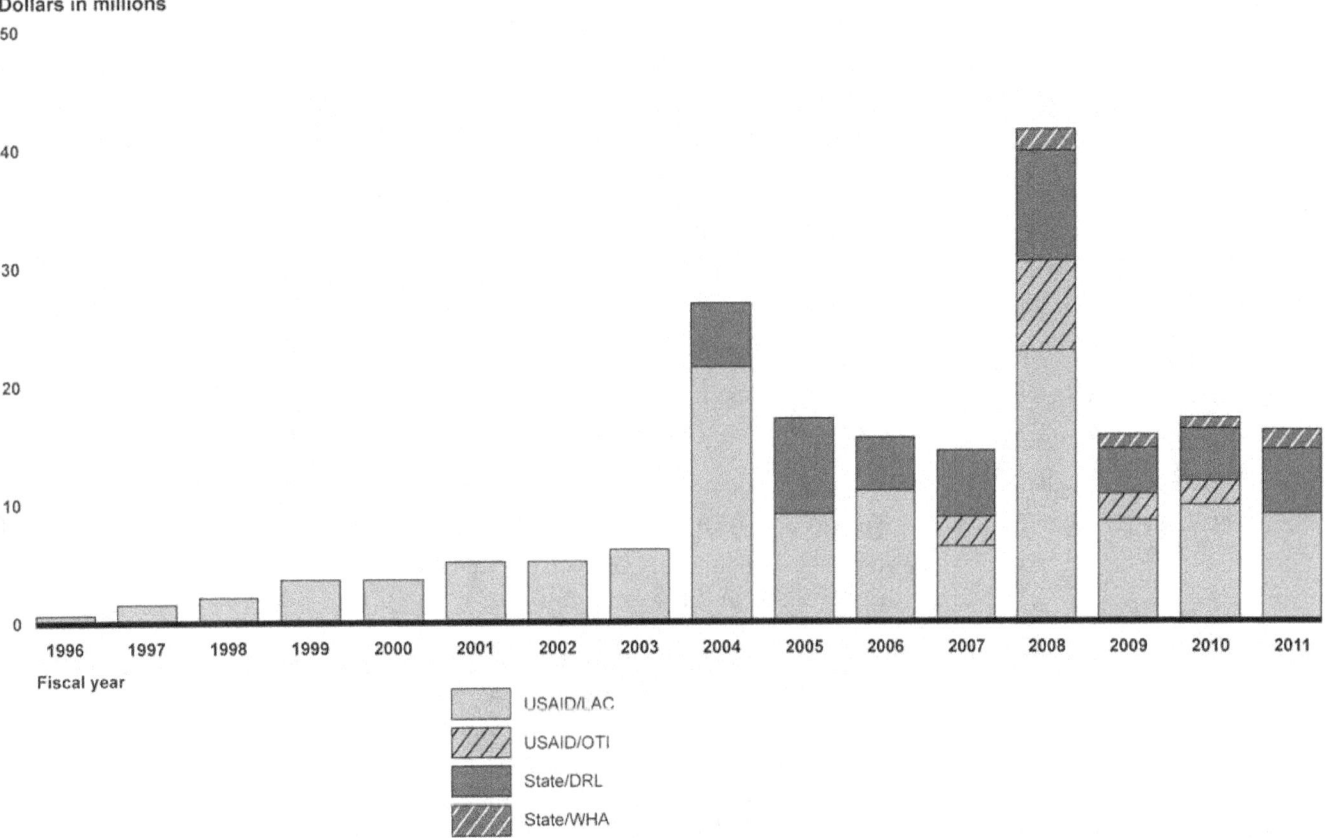

Dollars in millions

Source: GAO analysis of USAID and State data

Note: The fiscal year 2012 appropriations for Cuba democracy funding have not yet been allocated between the USAID and State bureaus. Since 1984, through its congressional appropriation, NED has also provided democracy assistance to Cuba ranging from $0 to $1.4 million annually from 2006 to 2010. In addition, since 2005, State/DRL has transferred funding to NED for Cuba democracy assistance that has totaled $14.4 million and has ranged from $0 to $4 million annually.

When the Cuba democracy program began in 1996, USAID was the only agency involved and USAID/LAC was the only programming bureau.

- USAID/LAC has received the largest total amount of program funding and has continued to receive the largest annual amount, averaging $12.1 million annually since fiscal year 2004.

- USAID/OTI received program funding totaling $14.3 million from the appropriations for fiscal years 2007 through 2010.[16]

State has received 32 percent of Cuba democracy funding since fiscal year 2004.

- State/DRL has received an average of $5.8 million annually since fiscal year 2004.[17]
- State/WHA has received an average of $1.4 million annually since fiscal year 2008.

USAID and State Have Provided Most Recent Awards and Contracts to Worldwide or Regional Organizations

USAID and State have awarded funding for Cuba democracy assistance to three categories of partners: (1) Cuba-specific nongovernmental organizations (NGO), (2) worldwide or regional organizations, and (3) universities.[18]

USAID's and State's awards and contracts tended to share certain characteristics, such as their broad objectives and amounts awarded, depending on the type of partner.

- *Objectives.* USAID and State awards and contracts to Cuba-specific NGOs and to worldwide or regional organizations have generally funded similar types of program activities, such as efforts to provide training and material assistance on the island. Awards to universities have tended to have different objectives. In the early years of the Cuba program, awards to universities funded activities such as research on how to promote a democratic transition in Cuba and

---

[16]USAID/OTI's funding supported the award and oversight of one grant and one contract. According to USAID/OTI officials, USAID/OTI does not plan to continue its Cuba program activities, which were envisioned from their inception to be temporary. The office's programs are generally intended to provide short-term assistance to take advantage of windows of opportunity to build democracy and peace.

[17]This average amount does not include additional funding that State/DRL has transferred to NED, which totaled $14.4 million from fiscal years 2005 to 2011.

[18]Cuba-specific NGOs focus only on Cuba; worldwide or regional organizations, comprising both NGOs and for-profit companies, focus on multiple countries. Although most Cuba funds have been awarded through grants or cooperative agreements to NGOs, USAID has also awarded contracts to two companies that operate worldwide. All universities that have received program funding are based in the United States.

scholarships to study at universities in the United States. Since the mid-2000s, after finding that the Cuban government would not provide exit visas for Cuban students to study in the United States, USAID and State have awarded funding to universities largely for programs to provide distance learning training to Cubans on the island or courses at universities in other Latin American countries.

- *Amount of award or contract.* USAID's awards and contracts in fiscal years 1996 through 2012 averaged $1.9 million for Cuba-specific NGOs, and $2.1 million for worldwide or regional organizations. State's awards and contracts averaged $0.8 million for Cuba-specific NGOs and $0.9 million for worldwide or regional organizations. Both USAID's and State's awards and contracts to universities averaged $0.8 million.

In fiscal years 1996 through 2012, USAID and State had a combined total of 111 awards and contracts to 51 partners representing all three types of organizations (see fig. 2). Many of the awards were concentrated among certain partners, with 25 of these partners receiving multiple awards from USAID, State, or both. For example, one partner received a combined 11 awards from USAID and State, more than any other partner, and 10 of the 51 partners received 67 percent of total funding to partners.[19]

---

[19]USAID and State awarded most program funding through cooperative agreements and grants, respectively. In terms of annualized funding, USAID's largest cooperative agreement was for $6.7 million over 4 years, and State's largest grant was for $6.1 million over 3.25 years. Only two contracts were awarded, both by USAID in 2008, one for $11.6 million over 3.75 years and the other for $6.9 million over 2.5 years. Since 2006, most USAID and State awards and contracts have resulted from openly competed solicitation processes.

Figure 2: Characteristics of USAID and State Cuba Democracy Assistance Implementing Partners and Their Awards and Contracts, Fiscal Years 1996-2012

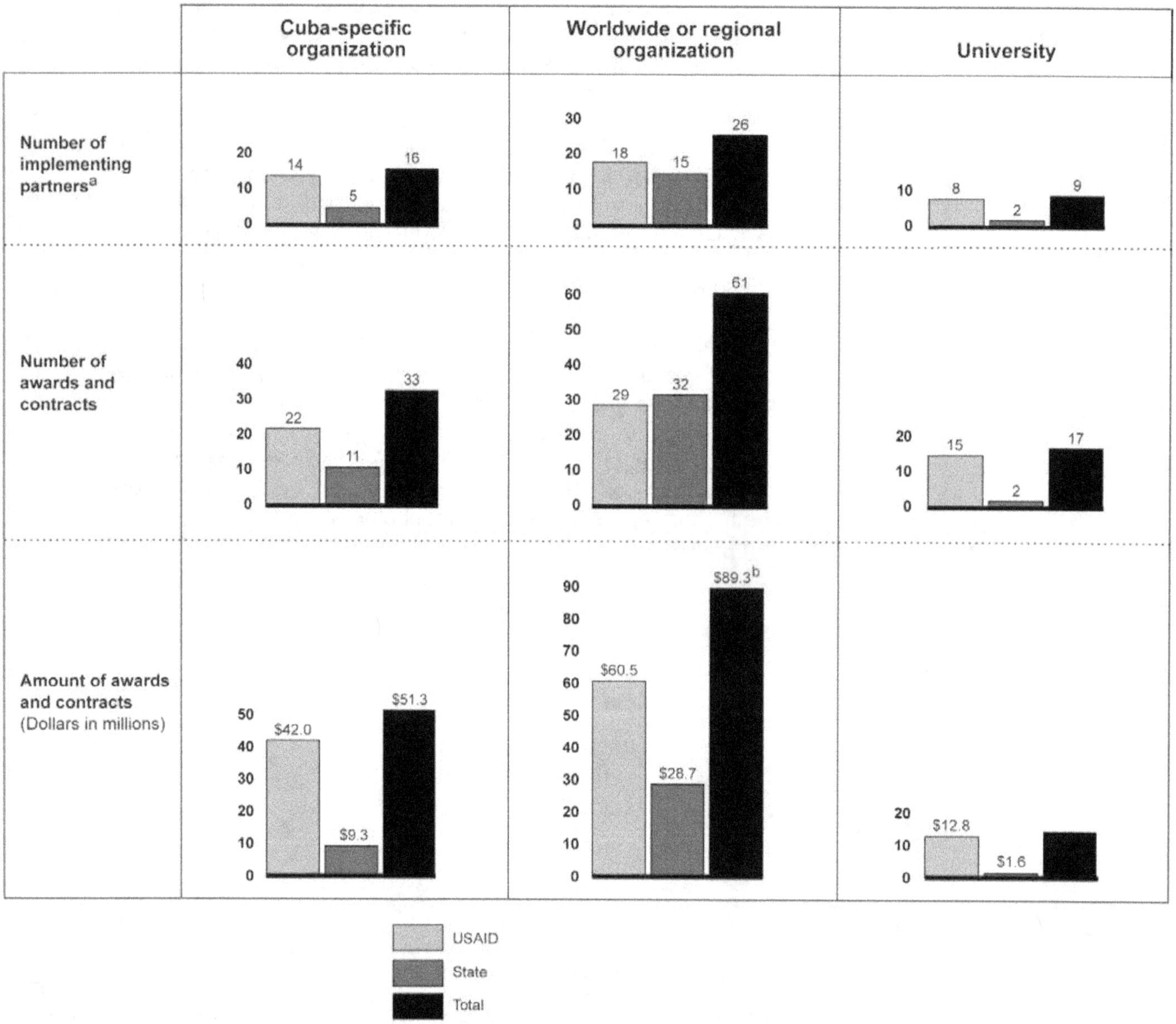

	Cuba-specific organization	Worldwide or regional organization	University
Number of implementing partners[a]	USAID 14, State 5, Total 16	USAID 18, State 15, Total 26	USAID 8, State 2, Total 9
Number of awards and contracts	USAID 22, State 11, Total 33	USAID 29, State 32, Total 61	USAID 15, State 2, Total 17
Amount of awards and contracts (Dollars in millions)	USAID $42.0, State $9.3, Total $51.3	USAID $60.5, State $28.7, Total $89.3[b]	USAID $12.8, State $1.6

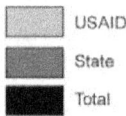

- USAID
- State
- Total

Source: GAO analysis of USAID and State records.

[a]The sum of USAID's and State's implementing partners exceeds the total for each type of organization because 11 implementing partners, across the different types of organizations, received awards from both USAID and State.
[b]Difference in sum of subtotals and total is due to rounding.

Since fiscal year 2008, regional or worldwide organizations have had more active USAID and State awards and contracts each year, and have received more funding, than Cuba-specific NGOs or universities. Prior to 2008, Cuba-specific NGOs had more active USAID awards than the other categories of recipients in most years. However, the program's partners have consistently included worldwide or regional organizations, some of which have a history of working on Cuba issues (see fig. 3). For example, for awards that began in fiscal years 1996 through 2007, Cuba-specific NGOs received 48 percent of award funding, worldwide or regional organizations received 43 percent, and universities received 9 percent. In contrast, for awards made since fiscal year 2008, worldwide or regional organizations received 74 percent of award and contract funding, while Cuba-specific NGOs received almost 17 percent, and universities received almost 10 percent. As we previously reported, this greater use of worldwide or regional organizations, which began in 2008, reflected more formal requirements for submitting proposals and USAID's decision to fund awards and contracts that incorporate capacity building for subpartners as an important element.[20]

___

[20]GAO-09-165.

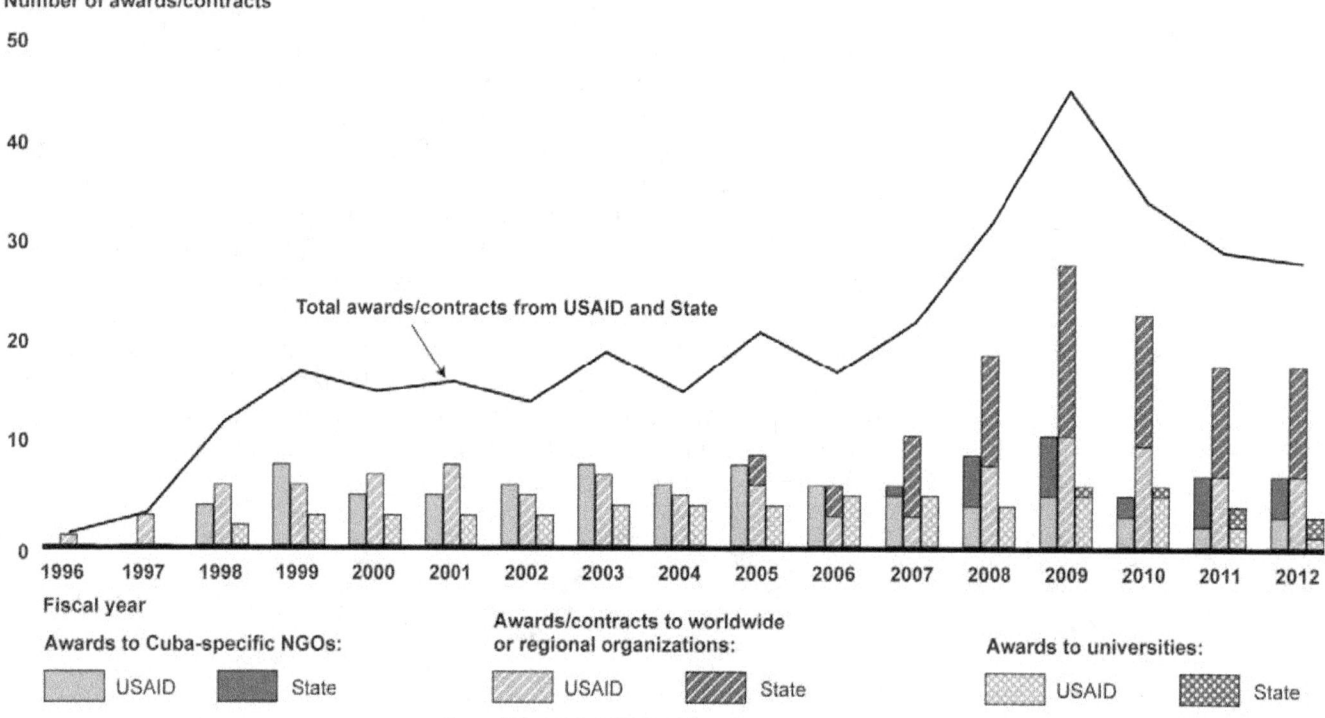

Figure 3: Number of Active USAID and State Awards and Contracts for Cuba Democracy Assistance, by Type of Organization, Fiscal Years 1996-2012

Source: GAO analysis of USAID and State data.

Most Partners Use Subpartners to Help Implement Program Activities

Many partners, and worldwide or regional organizations in particular, use subpartners to help carry out their Cuba democracy assistance work. We reviewed 29 recent awards and contracts to determine the extent to which partners use subpartners to implement program activities.[21] We found that partners used subpartners under 21 of the 29 awards and contracts, obligating about 40 percent of the funding under these awards and contracts to subpartners. On average, partners that used subpartners under an award or contract had 12 subpartners.

[21]We reviewed selected characteristics—including the use of subpartners—for all of USAID's and State's 29 awards and contracts that were active in fiscal year 2011, funded with appropriations from fiscal years 2007 through 2009. These awards and contracts were awarded to 22 partners.

However, the numbers of subpartners under each of the 21 awards varied:

- Four awards had one subpartner.
- Seven awards had between two and nine subpartners.
- Ten awards and contracts had more than 10 and up to 38 subpartners.

The purposes of subawards and subcontracts also varied greatly. Many subawards and subcontracts were for discrete activities, such as to conduct workshops. Other subawards and subcontracts covered an array of tasks, such as content development and instruction for a distance learning course or development, training, and support for civil society networks. Accordingly, subpartners included different types of non-profit and for-profit organizations as well as individuals who worked as consultants that provided the skills necessary to implement the varying activities.

Furthermore, the amount of funding that went to subpartners ranged from less than $5,000 to several hundred thousand dollars. For six of the 21 awards and contracts with subpartners, the majority of program funding was obligated to subpartners. In such cases, subpartners generally performed all or most of the programmatic functions under the overall award or contract, while the partners' main functions were to provide strategic direction of the overall award or contract and to perform management functions such as reporting to the agency and overseeing their subpartners.

Worldwide or regional organizations were more likely to use subpartners than were the other categories of organizations. In total, 93 percent of the subawards and subcontracts were awarded by worldwide or regional organizations. Also, on average, worldwide or regional organizations had 12 subpartners for each of their awards or contracts, while Cuba-specific NGOs had three and universities had five. Correspondingly, five of the six partners that obligated the majority of their funding to subpartners were worldwide or regional organizations.

Agencies Exercise Discretion under Authorizing Legislation in Funding Cuba Program Activities

USAID and State legal officials view the Cuba program's authorizing legislation as providing the purposes for which foreign assistance funds may be used and allowing discretion to determine which program activities will be funded. The officials stated that they view the types of activities listed in section 109(a) of the Helms-Burton Act as illustrating, not limiting, the types of program assistance that the agencies can provide. Specific authority for Cuba democracy assistance activities was provided in section 1705 of the Cuban Democracy Act of 1992 and in section 109(a) of the Helms-Burton Act in 1996.[22] Section 1705 authorizes the donation of food for NGOs and individuals in Cuba; exports of medicines and medical supplies, instruments, and equipment; and assistance to appropriate NGOs to support efforts by individuals and organizations to promote nonviolent democratic change in Cuba. Section 109(a) authorizes assistance and other support that may be provided, such as published informational matter for independent democratic groups, humanitarian assistance for victims of political repression and their families, and support for democratic and human rights groups.

USAID and State legal officials said that the agencies ensure that program activities directly relate to democracy promotion as broadly illustrated in related program legislation. For example, the officials noted that the types of activities that fit within the scope of "democracy promotion," as that term has been broadly defined in various foreign assistance appropriations,[23] would be the types of activities eligible for

---

[22]According to USAID and State legal officials, the Foreign Assistance Act of 1961, as amended, is the primary authority for both USAID's and State's efforts to provide foreign assistance to promote democracy in Cuba. These officials stated that because of prohibitions on assistance to certain countries and other restrictions in the act applicable to Cuba, "notwithstanding authority" is needed to provide assistance to individuals and independent groups in Cuba to support democracy-building efforts."Notwithstanding authority" allows agencies to carry out activities abroad regardless of country prohibitions or certain procurement regulations, personnel regulations, competitive process standards, or other restrictions that would otherwise prohibit or restrict programming. Both section 1705 of the Cuban Democracy Act and section 109(a) of the Helms-Burton Act authorize the provision of assistance "notwithstanding any other provision of law." See 22 U.S.C. § 6004(a) and 22 U.S.C. § 6039(a).

[23]For example, section 7034(m) of the Consolidated Appropriations Act of 2010 (Pub. L. No. 111-117) states that the term "promotion of democracy" means programs that support good governance, human rights, independent media, and the rule of law, and otherwise strengthen the capacity of democratic political parties, governments, nongovernmental organizations and institutions, and citizens to support the development of democratic states, institutions, and practices that are responsive and accountable to citizens.

GAO-13-285 Cuba Democracy Assistance

funding under section 109(a) of the Helms-Burton Act. They added that, while the agencies have not compiled a list of activities that will be approved or not approved for funding under the Cuba program, proposed or approved activities are set forth in agency congressional notifications and listed in individual requests for proposals or applications and in award agreements and contracts. In addition, they said that organizations are expected to work with agency program officers to determine what activities are permitted or appropriate, and whether Department of Treasury and Commerce authorizations, as required, already exist for delivery of various types of assistance or whether the organization must instead apply for a license.[24] Furthermore, they noted that program partners and subpartners, including subpartners based in other countries, are expected to spend U.S. government funds consistent with U.S. laws and that requirements in primary award agreements and contracts generally flow down to any subpartners.

---

[24]Under Treasury regulations at 31 C.F.R. Part 515, general licenses authorize certain types of transactions in which Cuba or a Cuban national has an interest, such as certain humanitarian assistance, without the need to apply for a specific license on a case-by-case basis. By statute, informational materials may be exported to Cuba without a license. In addition, USAID and State legal officials noted that USAID and State/DRL both have specific licenses that may extend to implementing organizations and individuals under the program.

USAID Has Improved Its Monitoring of Partners; State's Monitoring Does Not Ensure Program Funds Are Used as Intended

Since 2008, USAID has worked to improve performance and financial monitoring of its Cuba program partners.[25] However, we found gaps in State's financial monitoring efforts. For performance monitoring, we found some deficiencies in the performance planning and reporting conducted by USAID's and State's partners in our nongeneralizable sample, but both agencies are taking steps to improve their performance monitoring. For financial monitoring, USAID has hired an external auditor to perform financial internal controls reviews of its partners, and has used a risk-based approach considering criteria such as award value and prior issues identified to determine the coverage and frequency of the 30 reviews the auditor has conducted. These reviews have identified financial management, procurement, and internal controls weaknesses that USAID has taken steps to address. While State conducted no financial internal controls reviews for at least two-thirds of its partners between fiscal year 2010 and 2012, State recently hired an external auditor to perform such reviews starting in fiscal year 2013 and has taken steps to implement a risk-based approach to prioritize the scheduling of its reviews. Specifically, State plans to complete reviews for three-quarters of State/DRL's partners and none of State/WHA's partners. In addition, in accordance with federal regulations, the agencies approve partner requests to award funding to specific subpartners. In June 2011, USAID provided specific written guidance to its partners on what USAID requires for approval of subpartners. State has provided limited written guidance on approval to some partners, which does not clearly inform partners of the specific types of information State requires for approval. As a result, State was not provided with the detailed information that officials told us would have been required for State to have approved 91 subawards and subcontracts that were obligated under eight of its recent awards.

---

[25]We selected a nonprobability, nongeneralizable sample of six USAID and State implementing partners and 11 of their subpartners, to assess performance and financial monitoring and oversight of their awards and contracts. These six partners were among the top 15 recipients of program funding awarded in fiscal years 2007 through 2010 and represented about 60 percent of funding for awards active in fiscal year 2011.

USAID and State Are Taking Steps to Improve Their Performance Monitoring to Address Weaknesses in Some Partners' Performance Planning and Reporting

USAID Continues to Take Steps to Improve Performance Monitoring; USAID's Partners' Had Some Weaknesses in Performance Planning

USAID's Performance Monitoring of Implementing Partners

Sources: GAO analysis of USAID and State data; Nova Development (clip art); and Corel Graphics (logos).

USAID has taken steps to improve its ability to monitor its Cuba program partners' performance, by working with them to improve their performance planning and reporting.[26] USAID has numerous requirements for partners' performance planning and reporting, the key elements of which are summarized below.

- **Performance Planning:** USAID directs its Cuba program partners to establish monitoring and evaluation (M/E) plans that include certain specific characteristics.[27] USAID works with partners to include more detailed information on indicators in their M/E plans. USAID/LAC also required its one contractor to perform data quality assessments on its performance data.

- **Performance Reporting:** USAID requires awardees to submit progress reports on a quarterly basis and requires contractors to submit monthly and annual progress reports, among others.[28] USAID uses information in these performance reports to track the progress of individual awards and contracts and to track the progress of the overall Cuba program. According to USAID officials, USAID first reviews the reporting to compare it against targets set in partners' M/E plans. In addition, USAID analyzes and aggregates the information reported by partners to track performance for USAID's Cuba program

---

[26]The statutory framework for performance management of U.S. government programs is contained in the Government Performance and Results Act of 1993 (GPRA), Pub. L. No. 103-62, as amended by the GPRA Modernization Act of 2010, Pub. L. No. 111-352.

[27]USAID now uses the term "performance management plan" to refer to monitoring and evaluation plans. USAID regulations require that every country program and its partners develop and maintain a comprehensive performance management system.

[28]According to USAID regulations, these reports should compile information about activities that occurred under the award or contract during the reporting period, including any activities carried out by subpartners, if applicable.

and to report to State's Office of U.S. Foreign Assistance Resources on government-wide performance.

We reviewed the M/E plans and progress reports for the five USAID awards or contracts in our nongeneralizable sample, which began in fiscal year 2008 or 2009 (see table 3).[29] We found some weaknesses in the partners' M/E plans but found detailed reporting against indicators in the progress reports we reviewed. For example, our analysis indicates that all M/E plans we reviewed included clearly defined indicators for program activities.

However, not all partners specified targets and data collection methods for each indicator in their M/E plans. Establishing targets for indicators during the planning stage is important because targets form the standard against which actual results will be compared and assessed. Specifying data collection methods for each indicator enables the agency to determine whether it will be realistic for the partner to measure performance for that indicator in a timely manner. One partner included no information on data collection methods in their M/E plan, while another partner only included general information on their planned data collection methods, such as by stating that the data would be collected by subpartners.

Based on review of the partners' progress reports, we found that all partners in our sample reported to USAID on progress through quantitative updates against each indicator, allowing USAID to gauge the specific progress made during each reporting period.[30] One partner also reported progress for each individual subpartner, including by reporting the number of each subpartner's beneficiaries disaggregated by target group. Partners' progress reports also provided narrative information

---

[29]We reviewed M/E plans to determine if they had clearly defined indicators, targets set for each indicator, and data collection methods specified for each indicator, as these were some basic elements of M/E plans as defined in both USAID and State guidance. To review progress reports, we determined whether progress was clearly reported against each indicator identified in the M/E plans, as such reporting allows the agency to see the progress being made toward the awards' and contracts' identified objectives, according to USAID and State guidance.

[30]Four of the partners did this through organizing their reporting against targets into indicator tracking tables, while another partner provided weekly quantitative updates on progress against targets to USAID/OTI through an online database.

describing program activities, challenges encountered, and planned
activities for the next reporting period.

Table 3: Characteristics of Partners' Performance Planning and Reporting for Selected USAID Awards and Contracts

| Partner | Awarding agency and bureau/ office | Performance Planning: M/E plans | | | Performance reporting: progress reports |
		Indicators clearly defined	Target set for each indicator	Data collection methods identified for each indicator	Updates on progress clearly reported for each indicator
Partner #1	USAID/OTI	●	○	◡	●
Partner #2	USAID/LAC	●	◡	●	●
Partner #3	USAID/LAC	●	○	○	●
Partner #4	USAID/LAC	●	●	●	●
Partner #5	USAID/LAC	●	●	●	●

Legend: ● = Yes; ◡ = Partially; ○ = No.

Source: GAO analysis of USAID and partner records.

Note: Each row in the table represents a separate award or contract. M/E plans for our sample partners were created in fiscal year 2008 or 2009 when their awards and contracts began. The progress reports we reviewed were from fiscal year 2011, except for Partner #2 progress reports from fiscal year 2009.

Although we found some gaps in these partners' performance planning, USAID/LAC has been working to improve the quality of performance information that it receives from its partners,[31] with a particular emphasis since 2010 on improving their M/E plans. To improve M/E plans and partners' reporting based on those plans, in 2010, according to USAID, USAID/LAC conducted in-depth assessments of each of its partners' M/E plans to determine whether they included indicator tracking tables, definitions of indicators, data collection responsibilities, data quality limitations, and other key information. Also, in September 2010,

---

[31]In addition, in 2007, USAID developed and began to implement a structured approach to monitoring meetings with its partners through which USAID collects information on partner performance, such as more in-depth information on activities and planning. Also, since December 2009, USAID/LAC has convened quarterly coordination meetings for all of USAID's and State's Cuba program partners to provide guidance and share experiences and program implementation strategies. According to USAID officials, since December 2010, USAID and State have also used the quarterly partner meetings to obtain information orally about which beneficiaries in Cuba receive goods and services, to identify any potential duplication of beneficiaries across partners. Since partners often consider the names of beneficiaries as sensitive, they do not generally include names or other identifying information about beneficiaries in their progress reports.

USAID/LAC hired an M/E contractor to work with each of its partners to further improve and standardize their performance management systems. The M/E contractor has worked with partners to identify and track the most appropriate indicators, including any applicable standardized indicators that USAID/LAC can aggregate across the partners to determine its own overall progress. In 2011, this M/E contractor also provided training to each partner and helped them to improve their M/E plans, for example by specifying quarterly targets and data collection plans for each indicator. According to M/E contractor representatives, partners' performance planning has improved, although additional improvement is needed in the quality of some partners' data. In fiscal year 2013, the M/E contractor plans to perform data quality audits of the partners.[32]

State Is Taking Steps to Improve Performance Monitoring to Address Its Partners' Weaknesses in Performance Planning and Reporting

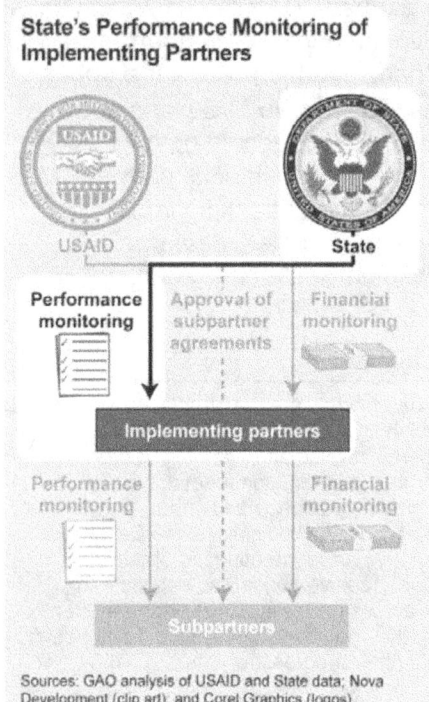

State's Performance Monitoring of Implementing Partners

Sources: GAO analysis of USAID and State data; Nova Development (clip art); and Corel Graphics (logos).

State has also made some recent improvements to performance monitoring of its Cuba program, in the areas of both performance planning and reporting. State's requirements for performance planning and reporting include:

- **Performance Planning:** State/DRL and State/WHA have provided different requirements for prospective partners regarding elements of M/E plans.

  - **State/DRL.** In 2010, State/DRL increased the level of requirements for prospective partners' M/E plans through the request for proposal (RFP) it issued that year.[33] Previously, State/DRL required that prospective partners submit an M/E plan but did not specify characteristics that the M/E plan should include. The RFP issued in 2010 specified that M/E plans should include a baseline and target for each indicator and data collection methods and sources, among other characteristics. In addition, the RFP referenced M/E guidance available on State/DRL's

---

[32]During these data quality audits, the M/E contractor plans to review whether partners document lists of specific beneficiaries counted against any particular indicators, either with their specific names or, given program sensitivities, some other form of documentation to show that reported numbers are accurate and do not include any duplication.

[33]Requests for proposals (RFPs) are used in negotiated acquisitions to communicate Government requirements to prospective contractors and to solicit proposals. (See The Federal Acquisition Regulation § 15.203.)

GAO-13-285 Cuba Democracy Assistance

website that included more details on how to develop an effective M/E plan.

- **State/WHA.** For the State/WHA award in our sample, the RFP issued in fiscal year 2010 required the prospective partner to submit an M/E plan outlining performance indicators, sources and means for verification, risks and assumptions for goals and objectives, and expected results and activities. For WHA's most recent RFPs issued in fiscal year 2012, State/WHA also included additional guidance for prospective partners' M/E plans, for example, including by defining indicators and providing a sample M/E plan. In addition, State/WHA further clarified that all indicators in M/E plans must include measurable, numerical targets.

- **Performance Reporting:** Both State bureaus require their partners to submit quarterly progress reports.[34] According to State/DRL and State/WHA officials, they review partners' quarterly reports against the partners' planned performance to confirm that the awards are making progress toward established targets and that activities align with the award's objectives.[35] State officials then analyze the quarterly progress reports to aggregate progress for each of its bureaus with USAID's progress to be able to report government-wide performance for the Cuba democracy program to State's Office of U.S. Foreign Assistance Resources.

State's partners that we reviewed ranged in the amount and kind of detail they included in their M/E plans as well as in their progress reports. For the State awards in our sample, we found that State/WHA's partner had the most clearly defined M/E plan (see table 4). This partner's M/E plan included specific and clearly defined indicators, targets against which the partner could measure its performance, and clear plans for data

---

[34]Similar to the progress reports submitted to USAID, State's partners must submit reports that compile information about all activities that occurred under their award during that quarter, including any activities carried out by subpartners, if applicable. Also, State officials may follow up with partners for more information by phone, e-mail, or, less frequently, in-person meetings.

[35]In addition, USINT officials will review the quarterly reports for these awards to ensure they are accurate.

GAO-13-285 Cuba Democracy Assistance

collection. For the four State/DRL awards, the partners included indicators in their M/E plans but did not define them.[36]

We also found that one partner with three State/DRL awards did not set clear targets for a number of its indicators. In addition, two partners identified some data collection methods in their M/E plans, but did not clearly identify which methods would be used to collect data for each individual indicator.

We also found that, for State/WHA's award, progress reports included detailed reporting against each indicator, as well as additional qualitative and quantitative information on overall progress including survey results and statistics. On the other hand, reporting for the State/DRL awards lacked such detail. For example, for one State/DRL award, the partner tracked its performance in quarterly reports for only 3 of the more than 10 indicators in its M/E plan. For three other awards, the partner did not aggregate or track performance against any specific indicators in their progress reports. While not reporting on progress against specific indicators, these partners generally reported anecdotally on the topics covered in the indicators or scattered some performance data throughout their reports.

---

[36]One of the awards in our sample, the third award to Partner #3 as listed in table 4, originated from the RFP State/DRL issued in fiscal year 2010, while the other three State/DRL awards in our sample were from the RFP State/DRL issued in fiscal year 2009.

Table 4: Characteristics of Partners' Performance Planning and Reporting for Selected State Awards

| Partner | Awarding agency and bureau/ office | Performance Planning: M/E plans | | | Performance reporting: progress reports |
		Indicators clearly defined	Target set for each indicator	Data collection methods identified for each indicator	Updates on progress clearly reported for each indicator
Partner #3[a]	State/DRL	◐	○	●	○
Partner #3	State/DRL	◐	◐	●	○
Partner #3	State/DRL	◐	◐	◐	◐
Partner #5	State/DRL	◐	●	◐	◐
Partner #6	State/WHA	●	●	●	●

Legend: ● = Yes; ◐ = Partially; ○ = No.

Source: GAO analysis of State and partner records.

Notes: Each row in the table represents a separate award. M/E plans for our sample partners were created in fiscal year 2009 or 2010 when their awards and contracts began. The progress reports we reviewed were from fiscal year 2011, except for the reports for Partner #3's third award, which were from fiscal year 2012.
[a]One State/DRL partner (Partner #3) received three awards during the period of our sample, and we reviewed that partner's planning and reporting for all three awards.

In September 2012, State/DRL awarded a contract to a firm specializing in M/E, which could address such gaps in its partners' performance planning and reporting.[37] In the area of performance planning, State/DRL has directed the M/E contractor to provide training and technical assistance to its partners to improve their M/E plans, such as to ensure they include information on data collection methods. In addition, State/DRL directed the M/E contractor to develop indicators for all State/DRL partners to report on that meet or surpass data quality standards. This should allow State/DRL to more easily aggregate information on the overall performance of its Cuba program partners.

---

[37]No State/WHA partners will be reviewed or trained by this M/E contractor.

Partners Generally Monitored Subpartner Performance and Used Various Methods to Monitor Beneficiaries

Implementing Partners' Performance Monitoring of Subpartners

Sources: GAO analysis of USAID and State data; Nova Development (clip art); and Corel Graphics (logos).

The partners in our sample had various policies, procedures, and mechanisms in place for monitoring subpartner performance, which they compiled information on to report to the agencies.[38] We found that partners generally required subpartners to report on their activities quarterly or monthly, and at the end of a subaward or subcontract. Some partners also required subpartners to submit trip reports after any travel to Cuba.[39] Other monitoring practices cited by partners included site visits to subpartners and frequent communication via phone, email, or in-person.

Because of security concerns and limited on-site monitoring in Cuba, partners and subpartners use a variety of methods to verify the delivery of assistance to Cuban beneficiaries. Representatives from USAID's M/E contractor indicated that partners have had difficulty collecting and reporting data because of Cuban beneficiaries' reluctance to maintain and provide specific information in writing (e.g., timesheets, attendance sheets, or other documents naming beneficiaries). However, the M/E contractor has found that partners and subpartners often communicate with beneficiaries though various means. Similarly, according to representatives of partners and subpartners we interviewed,[40] some delivery verification methods they used included the following:

- having future travelers ask beneficiaries how they used assistance provided previously; and
- observing beneficiaries' use of assistance through remote or indirect means—for example, through articles published online that demonstrate that beneficiaries received training.

Partners generally aggregate information obtained from such methods in their progress reports to the agencies. However, in certain instances, the monitoring methods selected have limited subpartners' ability to track and

---

[38]Partners are responsible for managing and monitoring each project, program, subaward, function, or activity supported by their award.

[39]These trip reports documented information such as the purpose of the trip, locations visited, number of individuals receiving assistance in Cuba, details on assistance provided, and traveler assessments of the situation on the island.

[40]We interviewed 11 subpartners under the six partners in our sample, nine of which were under USAID awards or contracts and two of which were under State awards. Some factors that we considered in our selection of subpartners included the amount of funding obligated to and the type of activity performed by the subpartner. Table 5 in appendix I describes characteristics of the six sample partners and their subpartners that we reviewed.

report detailed information. For example, one subpartner reported on an indicator, the number of signatures on petitions, by providing data that it obtained over the phone (instead of through document reviews that would prevent double counting of signatures and allow for other data quality checks). In addition, USAID's M/E contractor has found cases in which data could not be transmitted in a timely manner, preventing reporting on activities in the quarter when they were implemented. As a result, both the partners and the agencies can have difficulty knowing the exact numbers and identities of beneficiaries in Cuba.

USAID Has Improved Financial Monitoring of Partners; State Has Not Consistently Conducted Financial Internal Controls Reviews

USAID Has Bolstered Financial Monitoring of Its Partners

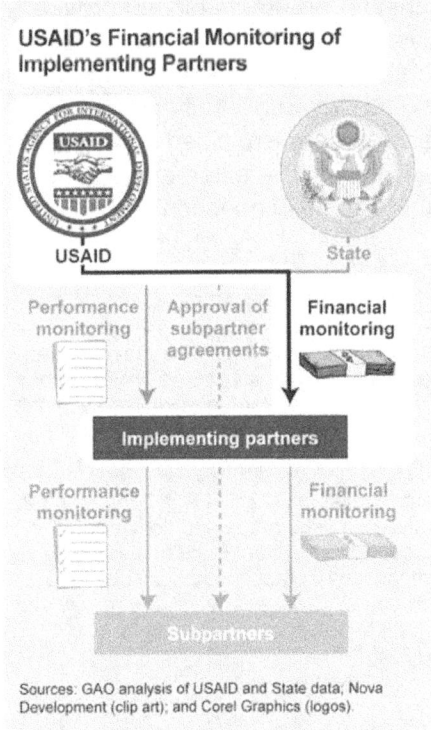

USAID's Financial Monitoring of Implementing Partners

USAID

State

| Performance monitoring | Approval of subpartner agreements | Financial monitoring |

Implementing partners

| Performance monitoring | | Financial monitoring |

Subpartners

Sources: GAO analysis of USAID and State data; Nova Development (clip art); and Corel Graphics (logos).

Since 2008, USAID has made improvements to financial monitoring of its Cuba program partners.[41] In April 2008, USAID/LAC hired an external auditor to perform financial internal controls reviews of its partners to ensure that they have appropriate internal controls and to review selected transactions under the program to ensure that they are allowable, allocable, and reasonable.[42] Since 2008, this auditor has conducted 30 audits across 13 of the 16 partners USAID funded during fiscal years 2007 through 2010. These audits are in addition to audits performed by USAID's Management Bureau and its Inspector General.[43] Across its

---

[41]We recommended that USAID strengthen its financial monitoring of its Cuba program in GAO-07-147 and GAO-09-165. According to GAO's *Standards for Internal Control in the Federal Government* (GAO/AIMD-00-21.3.1, Washington, D.C.: November 1999), for financial monitoring of partners, agencies' internal controls should be designed to provide for ongoing monitoring in the course of normal operations. Prior to 2008, the only ongoing financial monitoring that USAID performed during active awards involved reviewing high-level summaries of expenditures included in a standard federal financial report, known as Form 425, which partners submit quarterly.

[42]In addition to financial internal controls reviews, the external auditor has performed other reviews, as requested, such as compliance and financial systems reviews.

[43]USAID's Management Bureau performs preaward and follow-up audits. USAID's Inspector General also performs periodic audits of some ongoing awards and contracts.

different auditing entities, USAID has a goal of reviewing each partner approximately once every 6 months. Other risk-based factors are considered in the scheduling and sequencing of reviews, such as preaward reviews, prior audit findings, and period of performance.

Through December 2011, the external auditor had found 50 instances of unsupported costs, such as insufficient documentation and lack of authorization, and 15 instances of excessive costs charged to an award or contract, such as charging incorrect rates or expenses not allocable to the award or contract. In sum, the external auditor questioned 11 percent of the charges made to USAID/LAC during the external auditor's periods of review.[44] In addition, the external auditor found inadequacies in the following three main areas:

- the financial management systems at 11 partners,
- procurement standards at 8 partners, and
- internal controls at 8 partners.

Two of the external auditor's most common specific findings were that (1) partners did not properly complete their quarterly financial reports, and (2) partners did not perform a cost-price analysis before procuring a subpartner or equipment to ensure that it was procured at a fair price.[45] Specifically, the external auditor found that four partners did not provide any documentation of a cost-price analysis. In addition, the auditor found that another four partners had insufficiently completed or documented cost-price analyses, either by performing them verbally but not documenting them or by having unorganized or unexplained documentation of the cost-price analysis, limiting the external auditor's ability to confirm the reasonableness of the costs in question.

---

[44]At each partner, the external auditor reviewed nonpayroll disbursements that occurred during a certain review period, ranging from one quarter to over a year. As of September 2012, according to USAID, 75 percent of questioned costs were adequately resolved and USAID had received $50,000 in refunded costs, while the remaining questioned costs were in the process of being resolved.

[45]According to both USAID and State Department regulations (22 C.F.R. § 226.45 and 22 C.F.R. § 145.45), some form of cost or price analysis shall be made and documented in the procurement files in connection with every procurement action. Price analysis may be accomplished in various ways, including the comparison of price quotations submitted, market prices and similar indicia, together with discounts. Cost analysis is the review and evaluation of each element of cost to determine reasonableness, allocability, and allowability.

As a result of the external auditor's findings, USAID/LAC has provided training to partners and, according to USAID/LAC's external auditor, partners have made improvements. First, USAID/LAC asked the external auditor to provide briefings to the Cuba program partners at their December 2008 and March 2011 quarterly meetings on topics such as unallowable expenses, internal control standards, and procurement regulations. In addition, our review of audit reports issued from 2008 through 2011 showed that the external auditor found fewer inadequacies at some partners that had previously been audited. An official with USAID's external auditor who is responsible for these audits noted that recent reviews have found that the partners have improved their financial management capacity.

USAID/OTI used other processes to regularly monitor the financial performance of its partner under the Cuba democracy program. According to USAID/OTI, USAID/OTI staff worked closely with their Cuba program partner to plan future expenditures and reviewed documentation related to individual subpartners to determine each subpartner's real costs. In addition, USAID/OTI officials maintained a database that the partner updated on a weekly basis, allowing USAID/OTI to monitor all expenditures weekly.

Based on our financial internal controls reviews of the five USAID awards and contracts in our nongeneralizable sample (see table 5 in appendix I),[46] we found that partners' internal controls included (1) policies to prevent the commingling of U.S. government funds, such as unique accounting codes to identify awards and separate bank accounts for U.S. government funds; (2) policy manuals to instruct employees on the proper

---

[46]Our selected sample consisted of six partners. Out of the six selected partners, one had an award solely with State, three had awards solely with USAID, and two had awards with both State and USAID during the period from which we sampled. See table 5 in appendix I for further information on the six selected partners. During our review, we examined partners' policies and procedures, interviewed key officials knowledgeable of the partners' financial management processes, and then tested a nongeneralizable sample of transactions related to program expenditures under the partners' awards and contracts in our sample. Specifically, we verified that the transactions made were supported with adequate documentation; tested the partners' policies and procedures relating to approval of payments, segregation of duties, and subpartner approval; and reviewed the partners' processes to ensure that the payments made were allowable, allocable, and reasonable. We also verified that expenditures made were within limits approved in the contracts and agreements negotiated with the agencies and that payments made were in accordance with the scope of work established in those contracts and agreements.

use of U.S. government funds received through grants and contracts; and (3) procedures to segregate incompatible financial duties. We found that USAID/LAC was overcharged for some overhead and labor expenses by one of USAID/LAC's partners in our sample.[47]

State Has Not Consistently Performed Financial Internal Controls Reviews of Its Partners but Plans to Bolster Its Monitoring of Some Awards

State has not consistently conducted ongoing, in-depth financial monitoring of its Cuba program partners. State's Bureau of Administration is responsible for conducting financial internal controls reviews of State/DRL's and State/WHA's partners.[48] However, the Bureau of Administration has conducted financial internal controls reviews of less than one-third of partners active since fiscal year 2010. For State/DRL awards, the Bureau of Administration conducted one review in each fiscal year for 2010 and 2011 and four in July 2012. It conducted no reviews of State/WHA partners.[49] According to State officials, the Bureau of Administration attempts to conduct financial internal controls reviews at least once during the course of each DRL and WHA award but has not done so for many of its awards because of staffing turnover and constraints in the Bureau of Administration.

In September 2012, State/DRL awarded funding to an external auditor to perform financial internal controls reviews in fiscal year 2013. During this fiscal year, State intends for the auditor to perform one review of three-

State's Financial Monitoring of Implementing Partners

Sources: GAO analysis of USAID and State data; Nova Development (clip art); and Corel Graphics (logos)

---

[47]Specifically, we found that the USAID/LAC partner overcharged for overhead expenses, such as facility rental expenses and office supply purchases, because the partner included overhead in its labor rate multiplier (a negotiated multiplier applied to direct salary costs), while simultaneously directly charging these actual costs. We were unable to determine the total amount of overcharges caused by this double billing because the partner declined to provide us with information necessary to complete this calculation. In addition, we identified almost $1,000 in overbilled labor charges by this partner. In October 2012, we informed USAID of this issue.

[48]During the reviews, Bureau of Administration officials review financial records, documentation of expenditures, and the adequacy of financial and other administrative systems. The review allows State to trace financial statement balances through the recipient's general ledger, cash books, and other summary journals to the original detailed accounting transactions and their supporting documentation for audit trail purposes.

[49]Other than performing financial internal control reviews, State's main tool for financial oversight of its partners is to review the high-level summary of expenditures reported on their quarterly Form 425 submissions. These forms are reviewed by Bureau of Administration officials and officials in the relevant programming bureau, State/ DRL or State/WHA. State uses the information that their partners report on Form 425 to ensure that payments are commensurate with progress and that the partners do not maintain large unused cash balances.

quarters of State/DRL's partners and no reviews of State/WHA's partners.[50] State provided documentation to us showing that, in October 2012, State/DRL worked with the external auditor to develop a preliminary plan to select the ordering of its partners to be reviewed using a risk-based approach that considered criteria such as the value of awards, any prior financial compliance issues identified, and the partners' internal administrative capacity.

We conducted financial internal controls reviews on three partners with five State awards in our nongeneralizable sample (see table 5 in appendix I).[51] These three partners had been recently reviewed by USAID/LAC's external auditor, because they have also been USAID/LAC awardees, and had made internal control improvements in response to the auditor's findings.[52] Similar to our review of USAID's partners, we found that partners had internal control mechanisms in place, including (1) policies to prevent the commingling of U.S. government funds, (2) policy manuals to instruct employees on the proper use of U.S. government funds, and (3) procedures to segregate incompatible financial duties. However, State has had eight partners with nine State/DRL and State/WHA awards active in fiscal years 2011 or 2012 that have received no financial internal controls reviews during the course of their awards,

---

[50]The external auditor will review approximately 9 of State/DRL's 12 current and new partners.

[51]Our selected sample consisted of six partners. Out of the six partners we selected for further review, one had an award solely with State, three had awards solely with USAID, and two had awards with both State and USAID during the period from which we sampled (see table 5 in appendix I for further information on these partners). During our review, we examined partners' policies and procedures, interviewed key officials knowledgeable of the partners' financial management processes, and then tested a nongeneralizable sample of transactions related to program expenditures under the partners' awards and contracts in our sample. Specifically, we verified that the transactions made were supported with adequate documentation; tested the partners' policies and procedures relating to approval of payments, segregation of duties, and subpartner approval; and reviewed the partners' processes to ensure that the payments made were allowable, allocable, and reasonable. We also verified that expenditures made were within limits approved in the contracts and agreements negotiated with the agencies and that payments made were in accordance with the scope of work established in those contracts and agreements.

[52]Because of overlap in partners under State's and USAID/LAC's programs, nine of State's partners active in fiscal years 2011 and 2012 have been reviewed by USAID/LAC's external auditor.

through either State's Bureau of Administration or USAID's external auditor.

USAID and State Partners Used a Range of Mechanisms for Financial Monitoring of Subpartners

Our review of the six partners in our nongeneralizable sample found that partners had written policies and procedures for financial monitoring of their subpartners' use of program funding.[53] For example, partners had risk assessment processes to determine the level of monitoring required for a certain subpartner, depending on that subpartner's capacity and the type of subaward or subcontract. In addition, some of the partners required certain types of subpartners to provide receipts to document 100 percent of expenses.[54]

To test the partners' application of their financial monitoring policies and procedures, we conducted reviews of 11 subpartners under the six partners in our sample.[55] Generally, all partners maintained the necessary documentation (i.e., receipts, timesheets, authorizations) to support expenses incurred at the subpartner level. We found that partners maintained varying levels of documentation on cost-price analyses performed and that one partner had incomplete documentation for one of its subpartner's expenditures.

- For three of the five subpartners with fixed-price subcontracts in our sample,[56] documentation supporting the partners' cost-price analyses included (1) the actual amounts paid for similar services to subpartners on previous awards, (2) price quotes to procure supplies and equipment from various vendors, or (3) surveys demonstrating the market value of labor paid for different labor categories to substantiate that the amounts were within industry standards. For two of the five subpartners with fixed-price subcontracts within our

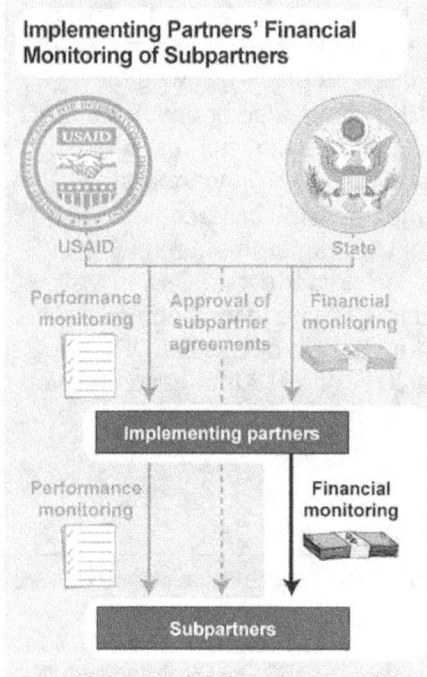

Implementing Partners' Financial Monitoring of Subpartners

Sources: GAO analysis of USAID and State data; Nova Development (clip art); and Corel Graphics (logos).

---

[53]According to Office of Management and Budget (OMB) regulations for awardees and Federal Acquisition Regulations for contractors, partners are responsible for financial monitoring of subpartners. Partners should manage and monitor the costs incurred by subpartners to ensure all costs expended are reasonable, allocable, and allowable.

[54]One partner noted that this 100 percent threshold was more than it requires of many of its subpartners, but that it maintained this requirement for its Cuba program given its high risk and monitoring challenges.

[55]For more information on these subpartners and how they were selected, see appendix I.

[56]The price of a fixed-price subcontract is set before the subcontract is signed and is not subject to any adjustment on the basis of actual costs.

sample, the partners documented that they believed the price of the subcontract to be fair based on the partner's prior experience.[57]

- One subpartner of a USAID/LAC partner submitted its receipts in a foreign language that staff at the partner could not read and provided little explanation of the receipts.

Agencies Have No Direct Relationships with Subpartners except to Approve Their Funding, and State Does Not Provide Clear Guidance on Subpartner Approval Requirements

Agencies Have No Direct Relationships with Subpartners Other Than Approving Partner Requests for Their Funding

USAID and State have no direct relationships with their partners' subpartners. Partners are responsible for all oversight of their subpartners and for reporting to the agencies any updates and problems related to the subpartners' work, such as through any quarterly reports and site visits. However, the agencies are generally required to approve any partner requests to award funding to subpartners.[58]

---

[57]We were not able to substantiate the assertions of these two partners based on the documentation provided. According to USAID officials, they are currently taking steps to address issues relating to lack of detailed information on cost/price analysis identified by USAID's external auditor for some USAID awards.

[58]OMB regulations state in 22 C.F.R. § 215.25(c)(8) that a partner shall request prior approval from the federal awarding agency for the subaward, transfer, or contracting out of any work performed under an award, unless described in the application and funded in the approved award. A similar agency-specific USAID regulation is at 22 C.F.R. § 226.25(c)(8).

USAID Provides Specific Guidance to Its Partners on Requirements for Subpartner Approval

USAID has provided guidance to its Cuba program partners on what is required for approval of subpartners, both during the preaward phase and during the course of the award.

USAID's Approval of Subpartners

Sources: GAO analysis of USAID and State data; Nova Development (clip art); and Corel Graphics (logos).

- **Preaward phase.** According to USAID officials, subpartners can be considered pre-approved during the preaward phase if they are described in award proposals, in accordance with the standard provisions that are referenced in partners' awards. USAID officials indicated that some of USAID's partners in the past had interpreted the term "described" to include any reference in a proposal to a subpartner's activities, even if the proposal did not specify that the work would be completed by a subpartner or provide specific information about the subpartner. As a result, USAID learned—through reviews conducted since May 2009 by its external auditor and its own subsequent reviews—that some partners had subcontracts and subawards USAID had not approved. In response, in June 2011, USAID added guidance to its requests for applications (RFA) on the type of information that partners must submit in order to receive prior approval for all types of subpartners.[59] This information includes, for example,
  - the name of the proposed subpartner,
  - a description of the work to be performed by the subpartner under the award,
  - the total estimated cost to be paid to the subpartner, and
  - a detailed, line-item budget.

  In some cases, USAID accepts this information orally if the partner is concerned that the leaking of this information could compromise the security of individual consultants who travel to Cuba. To provide further clarity to partners on whether or not USAID considers subpartners as approved during the preaward phase, USAID stated in its RFAs issued in fiscal year 2011 that a subaward or subcontract is not considered approved until the USAID Agreement Officer in the Management Bureau signs a letter approving it.

- **Award phase.** For USAID approval during the award phase, the partner must submit all of the same information as required during the

---

[59]An RFA is a type of solicitation notice in which an organization announces that grant funding is available.

preaward phase, as well as a copy of the proposed agreement with the subpartner and documentation of the process through which the subaward or subcontract was procured. [60] In May 2011, to further its understanding of the work to be performed by its subpartners, USAID/LAC set up a technical evaluation committee. For ongoing awards, partners submit proposed subpartners for approval to the committee. The committee may ask for information on proposed subpartner activities, among other things, to ensure that the programmatic content of the work to be performed by subpartners fits in the scope of the overall award.

State Does Not Provide Clear Guidance to Its Partners on Subpartner Approval Requirements

State's Bureau of Administration is responsible for approving subawards and subcontracts under State/DRL and State/WHA awards, and has requirements similar to USAID's. However, State does not clearly inform its Cuba program partners of these requirements in written guidance and, as a result, some partners have not provided the required information.

According to language in State's Standard Terms and Conditions,[61] prior written approval is required for any subawards or subcontracts unless they are described in the application and funded in the approved award.[62] Specifically, State officials told us that the Bureau of Administration requires certain information and documentation to approve subpartners, including

- the name of the subpartner organization,
- a copy of the draft agreement with the subpartner,
- the amount of and budget for the agreement,

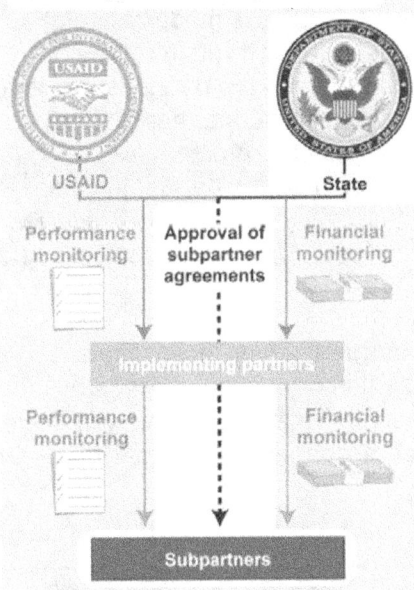

State's Approval of Subpartners

Sources: GAO analysis of USAID and State data; Nova Development (clip art), and Corel Graphics (logos).

---

[60]The USAID/LAC contract we reviewed required the contractor to develop USAID-approved guidelines, including criteria for selecting subpartners, and to obtain USAID approval for individual subawards and subcontracts. The technical proposal for the contract also stated that a USAID representative would participate in the contractor's subpartner proposal review process, and representatives of the contractor noted that they also submitted copies of all final subpartner agreements to USAID for approval. For the USAID/OTI contract, USAID/OTI worked closely with the contractor to select and approve all subpartners, in accordance with the contract terms.

[61]These Standard Terms and Conditions apply to all overseas federal assistance awards made by State.

[62]No differentiation is made in the Standard Terms and Conditions between requirements for the approval of subawards or subcontracts, including those for the use of consultants to perform work toward award objectives.

- the period of performance, and
- a description of the subpartner's role.

According to State officials, State's requirements are currently the same whether a partner obtains preapproval during the preaward phase or during the course of the award. They added that, for consultants under State/DRL awards, the Bureau of Administration does not require their names because of security and sensitivity concerns. Instead, according to officials, the Bureau of Administration requires information on the amount of the consultancy contract, the consultant's budget, and a description of the consultant's role and qualifications.[63] Nevertheless, the detailed information that State told us is required to preapprove subawards, subcontracts, and consultants is not specified in written guidance to all partners. For example, in State's handbook for grant recipients, State informs recipients to provide in award proposals details on any subpartners, but does not specify the type of information to provide. In addition, based on our review of fiscal year 2010 and 2011 award documents, we found that in cases when State/DRL is made aware of a prospective partner's intention to have a subpartner through review of their proposal, State/DRL included a requirement in the partner's award to provide a copy of the agreement with that specific subpartner to State within 10 days of its execution. However, State/DRL omitted this requirement from awards for which it was not clear the partner intended to use a subpartner. As a result, we found that many partners only received the broad written guidance in State's Standard Terms and Conditions and recipient handbook.

Based on our analysis of the use of subpartners under recent State awards,[64] we found that State had sufficient information to preapprove the subawards and subcontracts under State/WHA's awards. However, State did not have the detailed information that, according to State officials,

---

[63] These requirements for preapproval of consultants reflect factors contained in OMB, *Circular A-122: Cost Principles for Non-profit Organizations*, which lays out the types of information that an agency may use to determine that consultant fees are reasonable and allowable under an award, such as the nature and scope of the service to be performed, the qualifications of the individual or organization performing the service, and their customary fees.

[64] We reviewed the 18 awards that were State's portion of the 29 Cuba program awards and contracts funded from fiscal years 2007 through 2009 appropriations that were active in fiscal year 2011.

would be required to approve 91 subawards and subcontracts to which partners obligated funding under 8 State/DRL awards.

According to representatives of one of the State/DRL partners, they assumed that State was aware of their subawards and subcontracts and considered them preapproved because the partners' proposals had referenced the types of work to be performed under the award by the subpartners. We found, however, that the partners' proposals only provided general information for all proposed subpartners, such as an estimated total cost aggregated for all subawards and subcontracts. The proposals did not specify information about individual proposed subawards or subcontracts, such as proposed periods of performance, a description of the work to be performed, or copies of draft subpartner agreements. Officials said that State has provided training to grants officers over time to ensure greater consistency in the application of preapproval requirements. However, we interviewed two partners with ongoing State/DRL awards, and both were still unaware of the information required for subpartner approval.

Conclusions

USAID has been implementing Cuba democracy assistance efforts since 1996, and State's role in the program has increased since it began providing assistance several years later, in 2004. More than $200 million has been provided for these efforts over the past 15 years, with recent growth in the use of worldwide and regional organizations that often use subpartners to help implement program activities. Despite ongoing challenges stemming from the difficult operating environment in Cuba, since our 2006 and 2008 reports, USAID has taken steps to improve its performance and financial monitoring of Cuba democracy program awards. While State has also taken initial steps to improve performance monitoring of its Cuba program awards, we found that State's financial monitoring was lacking in certain areas.

For performance monitoring of Cuba program partners, both USAID and State have required partners to submit program planning and reporting documents that the agencies use to monitor their partners' implementation of program activities and progress toward program goals. Although we found some gaps in these efforts, such as instances in which partners did not identify targets in performance plans, lacked clearly defined indicators, or did not report on established indicators, both agencies are taking steps to improve performance monitoring of their partners. Specifically, since 2010, USAID has used an external contractor to enhance its Cuba program monitoring and evaluation efforts. In

September 2012, State hired an organization for a similar purpose, with work on this effort slated to begin in fiscal year 2013.

To enhance financial monitoring, in 2008 USAID hired an external auditor to perform financial internal controls reviews of its Cuba program partners and used a risk-based approach to determine how often each partner should be reviewed to enable more efficient and effective reviews, with resources focused on areas of greater risk. Such an approach considers key factors such as the value of awards, coverage, previously identified deficiencies, award type, and the frequency of the reviews that will be needed. USAID's auditor conducted 30 audits through fiscal year 2012, which identified questionable charges and weaknesses in partners' financial management, procurement standards, and internal controls. State did not conduct financial internal controls reviews for more than two-thirds of its awards during fiscal years 2010 through 2012, although State recently awarded funding to an external auditor for this purpose and has taken steps toward implementing a risk-based approach for these reviews. However, because these actions were taken recently, State's ability to ensure that funds are being spent as intended remains unknown until it has completed these reviews. Moreover, unlike USAID, State has not provided clear guidance to its partners regarding requirements for subpartner approval. As a result, State lacks complete and accurate information on its partners' use of subpartners to implement program efforts. Without adequate information on program subpartners, State has limited ability to fully understand and assess its partners' use of program funds.

Recommendations for Executive Action

To strengthen State's ability to monitor the use of Cuba democracy program funds, we recommend that the Secretary of State take the following two actions:

- To enhance financial oversight, use a risk-based approach for program audits, including those conducted by an external auditor, that considers, among other factors, specific indicators—such as value of awards, prior deficiencies, oversight coverage, and frequency—for each of State's Cuba program partners.

- To obtain sufficient information to approve implementing partners' use of subpartners, provide clear guidance to implementing partners regarding requirements for approval of the use of subpartners, and monitor implementing partners to ensure that they adhere to these requirements.

Agency Comments and Our Evaluation

We provided a draft of this report to USAID and State for review and comment. Their written comments are reproduced in appendixes II and III, respectively. USAID noted that it is a challenge to implement assistance programs in countries where USAID does not have dedicated staff in-country, and cited their ongoing commitment to ensuring that Cuba democracy assistance programs managed by USAID receive appropriate management and oversight to minimize waste and mismanagement and maximize impact on the ground in Cuba. USAID highlighted steps that the agency has taken to improve program management, such as dedicating additional resources to conduct financial audits and monitoring of awardees, and conducting pre-award audits on organizations with limited or no experience managing USAID-funded projects. USAID expressed appreciation for our recognition of the agency's program improvements.

State concurred with both of our recommendations and noted relevant actions it has taken or plans to take. Regarding our recommendation to enhance financial oversight through using a risk-based approach for Cuba program audits, State noted that the external auditor that State/DRL recently procured to audit some of its partners has taken steps to implement a risk-based approach. State further noted that the department is evaluating staffing in its Bureau of Administration and audit requirements to be able to address program oversight needs not covered by this external auditor. State also concurred with our recommendation to obtain sufficient information to approve implementing partners' use of subpartners. State said that it plans to hold meetings with awardees to discuss award requirements and provide an orientation on resources and technical support available to Cuba program awardees.

USAID and State also provided technical comments that we have incorporated, as appropriate.

We are sending copies of this report to the Administrator of USAID, the Secretary of State, appropriate congressional committees, and other interested parties. In addition, the report will be available at no charge on GAO's website at http://www.gao.gov.

If you or your staff have any questions about this report, please contact me at (202)512-3149 or gootnickd@gao.gov. Contact points for our Offices of Congressional Relations and Public Affairs may be found on the last page of this report. GAO staff who made major contributions to this report are listed in appendix IV.

Sincerely yours,

David Gootnick, Director
International Affairs and Trade

Appendix I: Objectives, Scope, and Methodology

This report (1) identifies the types and amounts of democracy assistance that the United States Agency for International Development (USAID) and the Department of State (State) have provided to Cuba and characteristics of implementing partners, subpartners, and program beneficiaries; (2) reviews USAID's and State's efforts to implement the program in accordance with U.S. laws and regulations and to address program risks; and (3) examines USAID's and State's monitoring of the use of program funds. This report is a publicly releasable version of a prior GAO report, issued in December 2012, that USAID and State had designated Sensitive But Unclassified.

To identify types and amounts of democracy assistance, and characteristics of implementing partners (partners), subpartners, and beneficiaries, we reviewed congressional notifications, agency and partner documents and data on program awards and funding, copies of award agreements and contracts and any modifications, partner interim and final reports, and other key documents and data. We interviewed agency officials and partner representatives to corroborate information and data obtained. We also discussed Cuba democracy assistance with officials at the National Endowment for Democracy.[1] We reviewed amounts of assistance and characteristics of partners that received program funding in fiscal years 1996 through 2012. To test the reliability of funding data, we compiled lists of all funding that went to each partner and sent these lists to USAID and State for verification. In addition, we reviewed the use of subpartners under all of USAID's and State's 29 awards and contracts that were active in fiscal year 2011, which were funded with appropriations from fiscal years 2007 through 2009. These awards and contracts were awarded to 22 partners. We obtained information and data from each of the partners on their use of subpartners under the respective awards and contracts. For the purposes of our review, we defined subpartners as recipients of subawards, including subgrants, grants under contract, subcontracts, or consultants. To test the reliability of subpartner data, we compared information obtained from partners to agency information, and interviewed agency and partner officials regarding any discrepancies. We determined data on

---

[1]The National Endowment for Democracy (NED), an independent, nongovernmental organization, funds programs to promote democracy in Cuba through both direct congressional appropriations and with funding that it receives through State/DRL. NED was not included in the scope of this review, because it is not a U.S. government agency and because USAID and State provide the majority of Cuba democracy assistance.

program funding and on the use of subpartners were sufficiently reliable for the purposes of this report.

To review USAID's and State's efforts to ensure that program implementation is consistent with U.S. laws and regulations, and to provide guidance to partners and subpartners regarding program risks, we reviewed relevant U.S. laws and regulations and agency and departmental policies and procedures. We also interviewed USAID and State legal and program officials regarding program implementation and related risks. For selected partners and subpartners, we reviewed award agreements; contracts; and partner guidance, policies, and procedures regarding program security risks and travel security and safety. We also interviewed representatives of partners and subpartners regarding program security risks and traveler safety and security measures.

We analyzed reported activities and assistance delivered, and management and internal controls for a nonprobability,[2] nongeneralizable sample of six USAID and State partners and 11 of their subpartners, in order to assess performance and financial monitoring and oversight of their awards and contracts. While the results of our analysis of these six partners are not generalizable to the population, we selected this nonprobability sample to be generally reflective of other partners in the population and to cover a large proportion of the overall dollar value of aid. We selected at least one partner from each of the four USAID and State bureaus and offices implementing program assistance—USAID's Bureau of Latin American and Caribbean Affairs (LAC); the Office of Transition Initiatives (OTI) within USAID's Bureau for Democracy, Conflict, and Humanitarian Assistance; State's Bureau of Democracy, Human Rights, and Labor (DRL); and State's Bureau of Western Hemisphere Affairs (WHA). While there were in total 29 partners from which we selected, the six selected partners were among the top 15 recipients of program funding awarded in fiscal years 2007 through 2010, and represented about 60 percent of funding for awards active in fiscal year 2011. Other factors that we considered in selecting partners included the timing of the awards and contracts—we selected partners with awards or contracts active in fiscal year 2011—and other strategic factors, such as the type of activity planned under the award or contract and whether

---

[2]A nonprobability sample is not randomly selected, but rather is selected based on the use of a set of key criteria; also, it is not a large enough sample for findings to be generalizable to the full population of partners.

the partner had ongoing or new program activities planned for fiscal year
2012 and beyond. We judgmentally selected two subpartners for further
review under each of the partners, except for the one partner that only
used one subpartner. To select subpartners, we considered factors such
as funding received, whether the subpartner had recent activity in fiscal
year 2011, the type of activity implemented, and other strategic factors.
These subpartners are not generalizable to the population, but provided
additional program context and examples for the purposes of our review.
Table 5 provides additional information on the partners in our sample.

Table 5: Selected USAID and State Implementing Partners

Implementing partner	Awarding agency and bureau/office for each award/contract	Total obligation to award/ contract	Number and type of subpartners reviewed per award/contract
Partner #1	USAID/OTI	$11,600,000	Two subgrantees
Partner #2	USAID/LAC	$6,857,817	Two subgrantees
Partner #3	USAID/LAC	$3,300,000	One subcontractor and one subgrantee
	State/DRL	$591,000	—
	State/DRL	$500,000	—
	State/DRL	$837,053	—
Partner #4	USAID/LAC	$3,700,000	Two subcontractors
Partner #5	USAID/LAC	$3,000,000	One subgrantee
	State/DRL	$591,000	One subcontractor
Partner #6	State/WHA	$821,232	One subcontractor

Source: GAO analysis of USAID, State, and implementing partner records.

To examine USAID's and State's monitoring of the use of program funds,
we reviewed and analyzed performance and financial documentation and
data and conducted interviews with USAID and State officials, as well as
representatives of partners and subpartners in our sample. In addition, we
conducted fieldwork in Miami, Florida—where we interviewed
representatives and reviewed documentation at local partners and
subpartners—and at the U.S. Interests Section (USINT) in Havana,
Cuba—where we interviewed U.S. officials and partner representatives,
and observed WHA-funded democracy assistance activities at post. We
examined USAID's and State's program operational plans and
performance progress reports; agency and partner policy and procedure
manuals and program guidance; agendas and information presented at
quarterly partner meetings; partner and subpartner award agreements
and contracts; partner implementation, monitoring and evaluation (M/E)
plans; partner and subpartner interim and final performance and financial

reports; and audits of partner activities, among other documents and
data.

To review partners' M/E plans, we assessed whether each plan had three
of the basic elements of M/E plans, as described in USAID and State
guidance: (1) clearly defined indicators, (2) targets set for each indicator,
and (3) data collection methods specified for each indicator. We selected
these criteria since they were common elements that M/E plans should
have, according to USAID and State guidance. Because we focus on
assessing the agencies' and partners' abilities to monitor, not to evaluate,
the Cuba democracy program, we did not select criteria for assessing any
portions of the M/E plans related to evaluation. We analyzed each M/E
plan to determine the extent to which the plan incorporated each element.
For example, we determined that an M/E plan partially met the criterion
for clearly defined indicators if the plan had indicators but did not provide
definitions for the indicators. For targets, we assessed a partner's M/E
plan as having partially met the criterion if there were relevant targets
specified for some but not all indicators. For data collection methods, we
assessed the partner's M/E plan as having partially met the criterion if
data collection methods were only described for some indicators or if the
plan generally described data collection methods, but did specify which
methods pertained to each indicator.

To review partners' progress reports, we assessed whether progress was
clearly reported against each indicator identified in the M/E plans. We
determined that a partner's progress report met this criterion if the report
included specific updates on progress for each indicator, with any
progress for quantitative indicators (e.g., number of beneficiaries)
reported in numeric form. We assessed a partner's progress report as
partially having met the criterion if it reported progress in this specific way
on some but not all indicators. We assessed a partner's progress report
as not having met the criterion if the partner did not clearly report
progress on any of its indicators.

Additionally, we interviewed officials from the two organizations
contracted by USAID/LAC to conduct performance and financial reviews
of partners. We reviewed partner and subpartner internal controls and
related residual fiscal accountability risk, and also performed walk-
throughs of their disbursement processes and reviewed invoices and
other supporting documentation. We primarily focused our review on

compliance with internal controls standards relating to monitoring of program funds and to reviewing certain control activities.[3] We performed selected expenditure testing at each partner and subpartner in our sample, when applicable, to identify potential internal controls or financial management issues. We also reviewed our previous reports and interviewed experts to identify lessons learned and to better understand challenges related to providing democracy assistance for Cuba.

We conducted this performance audit from September 2011 to January 2013 in accordance with generally accepted government auditing standards. Those standards require that we plan and perform the audit to obtain sufficient, appropriate evidence to provide a reasonable basis for our findings and conclusions based on our audit objectives. We believe that the evidence obtained provides a reasonable basis for our findings and conclusions based on our audit objectives.

[3]See GAO, *Standards for Internal Control in the Federal Government*, GAO/AIMD-00-21.3.1 (Washington, D.C.: November 1999).

Appendix II: Comments from the U.S. Agency for International Development

Note: GAO received comments from USAID on November 21, 2012 for the Sensitive But Unclassified version of this report.

David Gootnick
Director, International Affairs and Trade
Government Accountability Office
Washington, DC 20548

Dear Mr. Gootnick:

I am pleased to provide the formal response to the Government Accountability Office (GAO) draft report entitled "Cuba Democracy Assistance: USAID's Program Is Improved, but State Could Better Manage Its Implementing Partners" ▮▮▮▮▮▮▮ for the U.S. Agency for International Development (USAID).

The enclosed USAID comments are provided for incorporation with this letter as an appendix to the final report.

Thank you for the opportunity to respond to the GAO draft report and for the courtesies extended by your staff in the conduct of this audit review.

Sincerely,

Angelique M. Crumbly
Acting Assistant to the Administrator
Bureau for Management
U.S. Agency for International Development

Enclosure: a/s

- 2 -

USAID COMMENTS ON GAO DRAFT REPORT
USAID's Program Is Improved, but State Could Better Manage Its Implementing Partners
(▓▓▓▓▓▓▓▓)

USAID remains committed to the Cuban people by providing humanitarian support to political prisoners and their families, building civil society and expanding democratic space, and facilitating the information flow in, out, and within the island.

We are pleased that the draft report does not present any recommendations for USAID. It is a challenge to implement assistance programs in countries where USAID does not have dedicated staff in-country and we appreciate your recognition of our efforts. While no response or further action is required from USAID, we would like to take this opportunity to underscore our ongoing commitment to ensuring that Cuba democracy programs managed by USAID receive the appropriate oversight and management to minimize waste and mismanagement while ensuring the maximum impact on the ground in Cuba.

As the current draft report notes, "Since 2008, USAID has worked to improve performance and financial monitoring of its Cuba program partners," we are proud of the continuous progress that USAID has achieved since your previous reports, "U.S. Democracy Assistance for Cuba Needs Better Management and Oversight" (2006) and "Continued Efforts Needed to Strengthen USAID's Oversight of U.S. Democracy Assistance for Cuba" (2008). USAID has instituted rigorous programmatic and financial auditing processes and made the following enhancements to program management:

- Ensured that all grants and contracts are awarded competitively;
- Hired additional staff in USAID Washington to manage the program;
- Dedicated additional resources to conduct financial auditing and monitoring of grantees;
- Instituted the practice of conducting pre-award audits on organizations with limited or no experience managing USAID funded projects;
- Increased coordination with Department of State including USAID-sponsored quarterly grantee coordination meetings to discuss program activities and eliminate the risk of overlap.

Financial oversight measures have led to the identification of $6.8 million in questioned costs. Of those amounts, $5.1 million in questioned costs have been adequately resolved; and $1.7 million in questioned costs are in the process of being resolved. Overall, there was approximately $50,000 in refunded amounts to USAID. Systematic monitoring and evaluation help us establish targets, monitor progress, and determine ways to improve our programs.

We appreciate your recognition of our program achievements.

Appendix III: Comments from the U.S. Department of State

United States Department of State
Comptroller
1969 Dyess Avenue
Charleston SC 29405

JAN 1 7 2013

Dr. Loren Yager
Managing Director
International Affairs and Trade
Government Accountability Office
441 G Street, N.W.
Washington, D.C. 20548-0001

Dear Dr. Yager:

We appreciate the opportunity to review your draft report, "CUBA DEMOCRACY ASSISTANCE: USAID's Program Is Improved, but State Could Better Monitor Its Implementing Partners" GAO Job Code 320959.

The enclosed Department of State comments are provided for incorporation with this letter as an appendix to the final report.

If you have any questions concerning this response, please contact Katrina Fotovat, Deputy Director, Bureau of Democracy, Human Rights and Labor at (202) 632-2105.

Sincerely,

James L. Millette

cc: GAO   David Gootnick
       DRL – Michael Kozak
       WHA – Liliana Ayalde
       State/OIG – Evelyn Klemstine

Department of State Comments on GAO Draft Report

**CUBA DEMOCRACY ASSISTANCE: USAID's Program is Improved, but
State Could Better Monitor Its Implementing Partners
(GAO-13-285, GAO Code 320959)**

Thank you for allowing the Department of State (Department) the
opportunity to comment on the draft report *Cuba Democracy Assistance: USAID's
Program is Improved, but State Could Better Monitor Its Implementing Partners.*

The Department appreciates the professionalism with which GAO conducted
program audit meetings, data collection, and analysis over the past year and
GAO's stated willingness to incorporate the Department's technical comments into
the final GAO report. The Department also thanks the GAO for handling with care
the sensitive details of the Cuba Democracy Programs.

The GAO's report makes two recommendations. The Department concurs
with both of them.

First, GAO recommends that the Department utilize a risk-based approach
for program audits. The Department agrees with this recommendation and notes
that it is already using a risk-based approach that considers prior financial
compliance issues, internal organizational administrative capacity, and the value of
awards. The Department believes that the utilization of a risk-based approach to
program audits is essential for effective financial oversight. For example, the
Department has already procured an external auditor to conduct such reviews
incorporating risk assessment and has instituted enhanced financial monitoring and
oversight through increased site visits and other mechanisms. The Department
also notes that the Bureau of Administration (A) has not been able to conduct
internal financial controls reviews as planned due to staffing turnover and
constraints, and is evaluating staffing and audit requirements to address oversight.

Second, the GAO recommends providing clear guidance to implementing partners
regarding requirements for approval of the use of subpartners, and that the
Department should monitor implementing partners to ensure that they adhere to
these requirements. The Department agrees with the recommendation and has
been taking action to address this issue since prior to GAO's sharing of the draft
report with the Department. For example, the Bureau of Democracy, Human
Rights, and Labor (DRL) and the Bureau of Western Hemisphere Affairs (WHA)

2

plan to conduct grantee meetings. Among other information, we will provide an overview of award requirements, including compliance with applicable laws and regulations, limitations on expending U.S. Government funds, and an orientation on resources and technical support available. The Department has also taken action over the last few years to improve the programming process and program monitoring, including hiring regionally experienced technically certified program officers. We have increased guidance and standardization with regards to monitoring and evaluation.

Thank you for acknowledging improvements in the Cuba program since the GAO's initial report in November 2006. The Department has worked hard to strengthen the program, which provides vital assistance to support the desire of the Cuban people to freely determine their own future.

Thank you again for the opportunity to respond to the GAO draft report and for the courtesies extended by your staff in the conduct of this review.

Appendix IV: GAO Contact and Staff Acknowledgments

GAO Contact	David Gootnick, (202)512-3149 or gootnickd@gao.gov
Staff Acknowledgments	In addition to the contact named above, Leslie Holen, Assistant Director; Elisabeth Helmer, Heather Latta, Joshua Akery, Laura Bednar, Beryl Davis, David Dayton, David Dornisch, Ernie Jackson, Crystal Lazcano, John Lopez, Reid Lowe, and Kim McGatlin provided significant contributions to the work. Etana Finkler and Jeremy Sebest provided technical assistance.